30119 025 868 62 3

MCL

D1100859

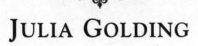

JULIA GOLDING

CAT AT SEA

EGMONT

EGMONT

We bring stories to life

First published 2007
This edition published 2008 by Egmont UK Ltd
239 Kensington High Street, London W8 6SA

Text copyright © 2007 Julia Golding
Cover illustration copyright © 2007 Tony Fleetwood
The moral rights of the author and cover illustrator have
been asserted

ISBN 978 1 4052 4185 4

1 3 5 7 9 10 8 6 4 2

A CIP catalogue record for this title is available from the
British Library

Typeset by Avon DataSet Ltd, Bidford on Avon, Warwickshire
Printed and bound in Great Britain by the CPI Group

www.egmont.co.uk
www.juliagolding.co.uk

All rights reserved. No part of this publication may be reproduced,
stored in a retrieval system, or transmitted, in any form or by any
means, electronic, mechanical, photocopying, recording or otherwise,
without the prior permission of the publisher and copyright owner.

LONDON BOROUGH OF SUTTON LIBRARY SERVICE	
30119 025 868 62 3	
Askews	Mar-2010
JF	

ALSO BY JULIA GOLDING

THE CAT ROYAL BOOKS

The Diamond of Drury Lane
Cat among the Pigeons
Den of Thieves
Black Heart of Jamaica

THE DARCIE LOCK NOVELS

Ringmaster

THE COMPANIONS QUARTET

Secret of the Sirens
The Gorgon's Gaze
Mines of the Minotaur
The Chimera's Curse

The Ship Between the Worlds

✒ THE CRITICS ✒

'London's greatest literary export since my own
plays went to America' – R. B. SHERIDAN

'A well-dressed tale of daring exploits'
– BEAU BRUMMEL

'Unexpected authorial manoeuvres worthy of
Admiral Rodney at his most inventive'
– LORD CHATHAM, FIRST LORD OF THE
ADMIRALTY

'She had me all at sea with her tale – water, water
everywhere . . .' – SAMUEL TAYLOR COLERIDGE

'England expects every man to read this book!'
– ADMIRAL NELSON

'We hold these truths to be self-evident: that all
men are created equal, but that Cat Royal is
possessed of a superior wit' – THOMAS JEFFERSON

'Enough to make you want to retire to
contemplate life in the wilderness' – HENRY
DAVID THOREAU

'Fancies herself a writer on Indian affairs? Well, I hope that's the last of her and her tribe' – JAMES FENIMORE COOPER

'Libellous scribbles, completely traducing the honourable intentions of decent American farmers' – GENTLEMEN OF THE LOYAL LAND COMPANY

'Her tales open up vast tracts of land in which the reader may roam free' – CREEK CHIEF MCGILLIVRAY OF THE WIND CLAN

'Sir, I am still too busy to read her – will you stop pestering me for my opinion. I have a country to run!' – GEORGE WASHINGTON

INDEX

⚓ Cat's Articles of War ⚓

Reader,

If you are about to sail with me, you should first read the regulations that rule in my navy.

1. All those in command of the English language are welcome aboard.

2. All persons on my vessel of war being guilty of profane oaths, cursings or other scandalous actions are in good company with the author.

3. Every person in my fleet who does not duly observe the standing orders of the admiral (me) to enjoy my tale is hereby ordered to go dunk their head in a bucket of seawater.

4. If any person in the fleet shall find cause to complain of the unwholesomeness of the fare provided, he or she shall quietly make the same known to his commander-in-chief who shall, as far as she is able, strive to take the criticism without losing her temper.

5. Care shall be taken in conducting and steering this vessel so that it be not stranded, or run upon rocks or sands, but keep an eye on the lifeboats just in case.

Your Commanding Officer,

Cat Royal

❧ PRINCIPAL CHARACTERS ❧

IN BATH

Catherine 'Cat' Royal – late of Drury Lane, your guide

Pedro Amakye – former slave, violinist, good at sea-shanties

Mr William Shepherd – crime lord who turns up like a bad penny

Frank, or the Earl of Arden – heir to a dukedom, under threat

Mr William Dixon – gentlemanly cousin of the Avon family

ON BOARD THE *COURAGEOUS*

Mr Syd Fletcher – press-ganged boxer, a faithful friend

Mr Maclean – purser and tormentor

Captain 'Barmy' Barton – unhinged captain, haunted by demons

First Lieutenant Lely – his humane second-in-command

Lieutenant Belsize – ginger-haired junior officer

Mr Harkness – friendly ordinary seaman
Mr Nightingale – burly bosun's mate
Mrs Foster – kindly gunner's wife

IN THE INDIAN VILLAGE

Kanawha – young Creek fishergirl, a mean shot
Tecumseh – her handsome warrior brother
Little Turtle – their shy amorous brother
Killbuck – their wise uncle
Grandmother Bee – an elderly medicine woman
with a sharp sting
Chief McGillivray – rich and wily leader of the
Creeks
Mr Davies and Mr Stuart – white explorers
recording Indian customs

IN PHILADELPHIA

Mrs Elizabeth Fitzroy, or Lizzie – an old friend,
grown rather fat
Mr Jonathan Fitzroy, or Johnny – American
citizen, proud husband

Dancing debutantes, sailors, Indian villagers,
etc., etc.

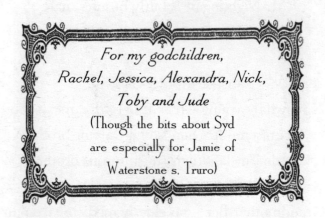

For my godchildren,
Rachel, Jessica, Alexandra, Nick,
Toby and Jude
(Though the bits about Syd
are especially for Jamie of
Waterstone's, Truro)

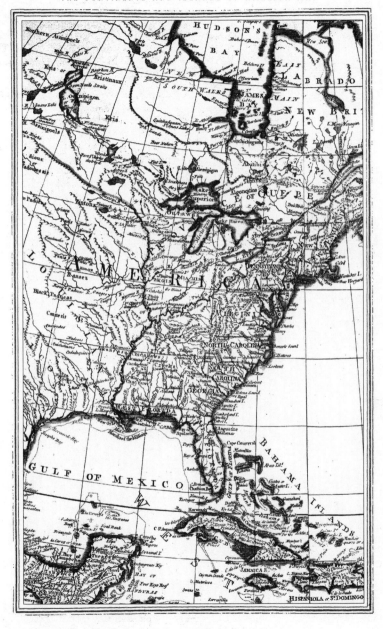

PROLOGUE
THE LIFE OF THE RICH

Reader, imagine yourself sitting in the luxurious surroundings of Boxton, the country house of the Duke of Avon situated near Bath. In the morning room, the walls are hung with hand-painted paper depicting Chinese flowers and animals; the delicate tables bear silver teapots and teacups so fine that the light shines through them. To amuse yourself, you have a pianoforte – or any other musical instrument you care to name, embroidery, sketching or polite novels. And what is the result? Boredom.

Do not mistake me, Reader: this is not just a little ladylike weariness – I am so bored I could scream.

My two friends, Frank, the Duke's son, and

Pedro, a superb violinist originally from Africa, are out hunting with the gentlemen. The duchess is still abed. And I'm left kicking my heels until the men of the family come home. I'd exchange an embroidery frame for a good muddy walk across the fields any day, but according to Frank, it would not be decent for me to go with the hunters. He even laughed when I suggested as much this morning.

'You know you can't do that. What would the other guests think?' Frank's navy blue eyes twinkled at me, daring me to laugh with him at my absurd idea.

'I don't care,' I said, refusing to succumb to his attempt to charm me into a good humour. 'I'll do something desperate if I have to sit about any longer.'

He smiled with slight apprehension, knowing me fully capable of acting outrageously. 'I trust you would not abuse our hospitality and do anything too scandalous. Take a well-deserved rest, Cat. Read. Study Latin if you must. You're supposed to be having a holiday.'

'No, Frank, gentlemen have holidays; ladies just have extended periods of vacancy.'

Frank cast an exasperated look at me, then turned to Pedro who was helping himself to a hearty breakfast from the sideboard. 'What shall we do with her?'

Pedro shrugged, piling three bacon rashers alongside a poached egg. 'Can't we take her with us?'

'Not you as well! You both know that'd cause a scandal.'

This was true: my position in the Boxton household was strange enough already. An orphan brought up in the Theatre Royal, Drury Lane, I had had the good fortune of making some unusually well-bred friends. When made homeless by the closure of the theatre, I had been invited to live among them while I sorted out my future. The invitation had stretched to several months. Pedro, just back from Italy where he had been on tour with his master, Signor Angelini, had returned to find me domiciled with one of the first families in the land; me, who had been the lowliest maid-of-all-work, now not even having to empty my own chamberpot!

'Act like a proper lady just for today, Cat,' Frank appealed to me, taking my hand. 'Some of my family have particular views about behaviour suited to your sex.'

'Not your mother, surely?' I protested.

He shook his head. 'No, she would probably tell you to put your boots on and take a gun with you. No, I was thinking of Cousin William. He's come up from Bristol especially for the shoot and to be introduced to my friends. I don't want him to meet you for the first time and get the wrong idea. I want him to like you; I want *you* to like him.'

Frank's cousin, William Dixon, had arrived late the night before. I knew Frank had been looking forward to this visit most among all the other company expected at Boxton for Christmas. He had described William with great affection, recounting many tales of previous holidays spent roaming the estate with them both getting into hilarious scrapes. According to Frank, over the last few years William had sobered as he had taken over his father's shipping business in Bristol and been deluged with new responsibilities, but I sensed that Frank still felt a little in awe of the glamorous older man.

On the strength of this description, I was strangely eager to meet him too.

'All right,' I conceded grumpily. 'I'll behave.'

'I'll stay with you if you like,' offered Pedro.

'No, no, you go. I'll be fine.' Given that Pedro was a former slave, it was important that the other guests realized that he was in the household by invitation, not as a servant. Staying behind to entertain me would undermine his status. 'Perhaps your mother will give me another singing lesson when she rises,' I suggested to Frank, trying to make the best of it.

Frank grimaced. 'You know her. She won't leave her bedroom till well after noon.'

'Then I'll find your tutor and badger him to translate a passage of Virgil with me.'

'Sorry, he's going on the shoot too.'

I sighed. 'In that case, I'll write to Lizzie

and Johnny and tell them what a scintillating time I'm having.'

Frank chuckled. 'You do that. Send them my love, won't you?'

'Frank, you really should write to your sister yourself.'

'I know, but you're so much better at that kind of thing, Cat. It's one of the female accomplishments that you possess in abundance.'

'Meaning I'm sadly lacking in the others?'

'Well, you could pass the time improving your embroidery – or painting a screen.'

I poked Frank in the ribs, making him spill his devilled kidneys on his lap.

'All right, all right: I surrender!' He held his hands up. 'And I promise I'll take you riding this afternoon when we get back.'

So there I was, marooned in the morning room, waiting for someone to rescue me. I couldn't remember being bored ever before. Life at Drury Lane had been so busy; something was always happening, what with the bustle of rehearsals, the noise of set construction, the daily ebb and flow of the audience as regular as the tides. And, of course, the excitement of each performance. I desperately missed watching Shakespeare and Sheridan acted out on stage. Despite having the library at Boxton at my disposal, the printed page was no substitute for a play. It was a madness worthy of Bedlam to expect anyone to be satisfied with Shakespeare from a book.

I was interrupted in my thoughts by the arrival of the post. Joseph, my favourite footman, brought me a letter on a silver plate.

'This just came with the carrier, miss,' he said solemnly.

This was a rare event: a letter for me. Thanking him, I turned the envelope over with interest as I didn't recognize the handwriting. After breaking the seal, I unfolded the cheap notepaper:

Bow Street, 1 December
Dear Miss Cat,

I apologize for taking the liberty of writing to you, but our Syd always said you were a true friend, so I hope you don't mind. As you know, our boy was expected back in

October at the latest from his boxing tour but we've had no word from him or his manager. His father and I are going almost out of our wits wondering what to do. One of Syd's boys suggested we write to you and ask you to beg that young lord of yours if he can make enquiries on our behalf. The last news we had was that Syd was in Bristol. They tell me that this is not far from you so I hope it won't inconvenience you to ask around for us.

Yours in hope,

Mrs Joanna Fletcher

I folded the note and sat staring at the walls, no longer seeing the painted paper but remembering my oldest friend. Syd, the gentle giant, leader of the Butcher's Boys, missing! I didn't like it, and yet I also found it hard to imagine that he could have come to any harm. He was too skilled with his fists to fall prey to anyone wishing him ill. There had to be an explanation. He couldn't read or write, so perhaps it was just that he was delayed longer than he expected and had failed to get a message home. Take into consideration that he was with Mick Bailey, his manager, then it wasn't surprising.

Bailey was a piece of work: I wouldn't put it past him to persuade Syd into staying away if Bailey was still making money from his boxing matches. Mrs Fletcher need have no doubts about us helping her: Frank and I would do all we could to discover Syd's whereabouts. After all he'd done for us, we'd go to the ends of the earth to help him if we had to.

An excited barking and slamming of doors announced the return of the shooting party. I stopped myself running out into the hall and sat demurely with the letter folded in my lap like a proper lady. Frank burst in, his face reddened with cold, curly brown hair hanging damp with dew on his neck. He looked full of energy, invigorated by his morning's excursion.

'Seven – I shot seven, Cat!' he said, rubbing his hands with delight. 'What do you think of that?'

'Poor birds, that's what I think.' I passed him the note.

The door opened again and Pedro entered, talking to a tall, handsome man who bore a family resemblance to Frank: same blue eyes and dark hair, same lanky frame, though his shoulders were broader and his nose worthy of a Roman emperor. It wasn't hard to imagine he might be Frank's older brother.

Frank frowned over the letter but thrust it into his pocket as his guests arrived.

'Ah, Will, this is the young lady I mentioned. May I present Miss Royal?'

Frank's cousin clicked his heels together and bowed most charmingly over my hand. 'Miss Royal, a pleasure to meet you.'

I rose and curtseyed. 'I'm very pleased you have joined us, Mr Dixon.'

'I hope my young cousin here has not been neglecting you?' Mr Dixon asked, ruffling Frank's hair affectionately. 'He kept us out far longer than expected chasing after an elusive eighth partridge.'

Frank grinned apologetically at his cousin. 'But Will reminded me of my duty to my other guests so it lives to see another day.'

With the newcomer among us, it didn't seem polite to ask Frank what he thought of the letter. Mr Dixon might not appreciate a duke's son being asked to run an errand for a butcher's wife. Frank obviously thought this too as he passed the letter to Pedro when his cousin's attention was engaged elsewhere. Instead we spent the time until dinner listening to Mr Dixon's lively talk.

'I have my own small business in Bristol,' Mr Dixon explained modestly. Frank had mentioned a far from insignificant shipping concern with vessels all over the world. 'It keeps me in this part of the country so I am thankful to have the delights of Bath to amuse me. I understand you like the theatre, Miss Royal?'

'Like' was too feeble a word for what I felt about the stage.

'Yes, sir, it is my passion.'

Mr Dixon gave me an encouraging nod. I realized then that he knew exactly who – and what – I was, but he didn't seem to mind. 'So I suspected, Miss Royal.' He flicked a curious glance at Frank and I wondered if I had misunderstood him. Perhaps he thought my background a mark against me? But then he returned his attention to me and my doubts melted away in the warmth of his expression. 'Well, you must come to Bath. We have our own very good little theatre; you'll hardly miss Drury Lane. And then there are the balls and the assemblies – Frank can't keep you tucked away here at Boxton, depriving the rest of us of your company!' He turned to Frank, tapping his arm with mock outrage. 'Cousin, I won't have it! You must prevail upon your mother to bring Miss Royal to the Assembly Rooms as soon as possible.'

I was flattered that Mr Dixon understood me. He seemed to realize what a torture it was to sit in the drawing room while everyone else was having fun.

'Oh, do, please, Frank. I'd love to see Bath,' I pleaded.

Frank looked to his cousin who nodded his approval.

'Of course, we'll all go,' announced Frank. 'See, Cat, I told you Will would cheer us up. Now, what about that riding lesson?'

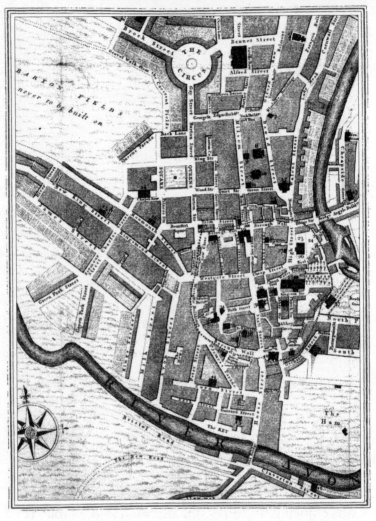

Act I — In which Cat tries to
remember that dangerous is Bad...

ACT I

SCENE 1 – DANCING WITH BILLY

F rank, Pedro and I agreed that same day to despatch Joseph to Bristol to make enquiries about Syd. After carefully preparing the ground to get Mr Dixon used to the notion that a duke's son counted a boxing butcher as one of his closest friends, Frank took him into his confidence and asked for his advice. As Frank predicted, his cousin's response was immediate and generous: he promised that his own people in Bristol would help with the search. He advised us to start at the docks: if anyone went missing in that part of the world, this was the first place to look.

'Why is that, sir?' I asked. We were at dinner. I had been placed on Mr Dixon's right hand and was enjoying his respectful attention at the table. It made a pleasant change. Frank was rather too inclined to treat me like a fellow, neglecting to refill my glass or offer me delicacies out of my reach.

This was all right in Drury Lane, where it was every man (or woman) for themselves, but at Boxton Frank did not notice that his behaviour often left me high and dry, with an empty glass and plate. I knew enough of table manners to be aware that it would have been unladylike to shove him aside to help myself. But Mr Dixon was not Frank; he was very agreeably different.

Mr Dixon poured a splash of wine into my crystal goblet, then watered it down. 'It is because of the press gang, Miss Royal. When they have trouble filling up His Majesty's ships, they go looking for likely customers and persuade them to serve their country for a voyage or two.'

I shook my head. 'Not Syd Fletcher. He's got his life in London; he won't want to go sailing.'

Mr Dixon smiled grimly. 'I'm afraid it does not matter what he wants once the press gang get him. He'll be thrown on board and expected to do his duty, willing or no.'

'But that's . . . that's slavery.'

'Not quite. He'll get paid and a discharge at the end if he survives. Who knows, he might even take to the life.' Mr Dixon must have noticed my shocked expression for he patted my hand. 'Do not worry, Miss Royal, your friend might not have fallen into the hands of the press gang. He might be quite at liberty, enjoying the life of a – what was it? – itinerant boxer.' He smiled at his cousin. 'My, Frank, you have got to know some interesting people while I've been away. I'm not sure I totally approve.' He quirked an eyebrow.

'I'm glad I've shocked you, Will,' Frank laughed. 'You never used to be so stuffy. My new friends will be good for you. They're all sterling fellows.'

'If they are anything like Miss Royal, then I'm sure I will be charmed,' said Mr Dixon, raising his glass to me.

There was nothing more we could do for Syd until there was some news, so I did not feel too guilty about enjoying the preparations for my first appearance in Bath. We had fixed on the dress ball the following Monday at the Upper Rooms and – guess what, Reader – I was to have a new gown!

Now, I expect my gentlemen readers to skip a page at this point, but, ladies, can you imagine it – me, a new dress! Not a hand-me-down from Lizzie's wardrobe. Not one chosen by someone else. But a completely new outfit made for me. You could have knocked me over with a feather when the duchess offered the services of her personal dressmaker.

'Don't mention it, my dear,' the duchess boomed when I had stammered my thanks to her. 'We'll look on it as your coming out.' Pausing for a moment, she tapped my cheek thoughtfully with her finger. 'You may be a trifle young for Society, but then you tell us you do not know your exact age. I think we can allow ourselves a little latitude. There have to be some advantages to being a duchess.' Returning to the game, she dealt me a card from the top of the pack, slapping it down on the table. 'And after all, you will be representing the Avon family: we can't have you disgracing us in a shoddy muslin, can we?'

Frank put down an eight of hearts. 'Sometimes, Cat, it's too easy to forget you're a girl just like any other. But after hearing you today go all giddy over bolts of silk, I won't forget.'

'Is that the best you can do?' I asked a shade resentfully as I trumped his card with a ten.

'Forgive my cousin,' said Mr Dixon, laying a knave on the top of the pile and scooping up the lot. 'I'm sure you'll do us all credit, Miss Royal.'

I eyed Mr Dixon as he gathered the winnings to his side of the table, already imagining myself on his arm, cutting a dash in the ballroom as we danced a cotillion.

And the finished dress *was* simply wonderful: made from a glorious patterned white silk, it had embroidered roses round the hem and delicate lace at the neck. Not too fussy. Elegant was what I was aiming for – and that was what I think I achieved as I examined myself in the mirror before leaving. I felt a twinge of guilt as I studied the exquisite needlework. I knew that a poor girl somewhere had probably slaved for hours over this – for very little pay. A number of my friends in Drury Lane had been seamstresses and it is thankless, eye-wrecking work, believe me. But, just for one night, I was going to pretend I was above such concerns. I was going to be a proper lady going to a real ball, just as I had so often done in my imagination. Who knows, perhaps I might even meet the man of my dreams and be swept off my feet? Why not? It happens in fairy tales and this evening it felt as if I was stepping into one.

I descended the stairs with the duchess to where the gentlemen were waiting. Her grace was robed in scarlet with a black feather nodding over her head, not unlike the costume of the Mogul prince Pedro had once worn at Drury Lane. Pedro caught my eye and grinned, knowing we were both thinking the same thing. Mr Dixon, dressed in a coat of dark blue – a colour that became him very well – stepped forward to take my hand.

'As I predicted, Miss Royal, you do us all credit.'

Frank, for once also smartly turned out, cast a strange look at me, making me wonder if I had got something wrong.

'What's the matter?' I asked, glancing anxiously at my feet. Two white slippers peeped from beneath the roses. I couldn't spot anything amiss.

'No, Cat, you look . . . you look very well.' Frank's face flushed as if he'd said something embarrassing. He then moved away from me and climbed into the carriage without waiting. Mr Dixon hurriedly covered for his cousin's ill manners by handing me into the coach as the duke escorted his wife. Frank was looking at his nails as I took my seat beside him.

'What's going on?' I whispered, completely baffled.

Seeing we were unobserved as his father made a fuss of settling the duchess's fur cape around her, Frank took my hand in its white kid glove and gave it a squeeze. 'It's just . . . you have to understand, Cat, I've seen you dressed as a boy, covered in bruises, as a ballerina, a Quaker, and all the time you looked like you. But tonight, you don't. You're someone else. It's . . . it's just a lot to get used to. I'm sorry.'

Suddenly I began to have doubts about the evening. Did I want to be this new person – this lady – that had shocked Frank more than any of my other guises?

But then the thought of my new finery bolstered my resolve. It wouldn't be like me to waste all this on a quiet night at home, now would it?

Mr Dixon climbed in and took his place on the other side. Pedro remained on the front steps to wave us off.

'Aren't you coming?' I called.

'Heavens, no, Cat,' he replied with a laugh.

'He's worried someone will ask him to dance,' said Frank, returning to his old self.

'No, I'm worried someone would shove a tray of drinks in my hand and expect me to play waiter all evening. The Assembly Rooms are no place for me.'

'But Pedro –' I began. The shine on my brilliant evening was already beginning to tarnish.

'It's nothing. You can't go shooting; I can't go to the ball. Fair's fair. You can tell me all about it tomorrow.'

Mr Dixon nodded his approval. 'The young

man is right,' he said. 'Sadly, he would only be despised for trying to move in circles above his station.'

The carriage moved off. I was silent, my thoughts employed cursing the world that constantly threw up so many barriers in the way of Pedro and me. Why couldn't we just be allowed to be ourselves – not a black boy or a poor lower class girl? It was almost as if we had labels round our necks proclaiming our inadequacy. Fittingly, it was at that moment that the duchess handed me a folded card on a ribbon.

'What's this?' I asked, turning it over.

'It's your price tag,' said Frank, fastening it to my wrist for me. 'All the single ladies carry them. Two thousand a year in bonds. Only child of ailing banker. Fifty pounds a year.'

'Frank, don't tease Miss Royal,' scolded the duke, frowning.

'It's your dance card,' explained Mr Dixon. 'And I've no doubt, dressed as you are, it will be full by the end of the evening and you will have worn out those slippers of yours.'

I was grateful to him for taking pity on my ignorance, but I also noted that neither he nor Frank rushed to be the first to be marked down on my card. Such depressing thoughts were pushed aside, however, as the carriage was beginning its steep descent of Lansdown Hill, giving me my first glimpse of Bath. Night had fallen but in many ways that only made it more exciting as the lights in the windows glimmered like a swarm of fireflies in the valley, allowing my imagination to fill in the details of the handsome houses and parades of shops I had heard so much about. The townsfolk had gone to a lot of trouble to build Bath to the heights of modern elegance, putting other cities to shame with their hotch-potch of styles. Where I come from in London, there has been only fitful planning as the city expands, leaving many streets with the more decrepit buildings slumped against recent additions. In Bath, the citizens have not been so sentimental, clearing the way for construction on a scale never seen before. The grand houses either side of the carriage bore witness to this: honey-coloured terraces clustered together to impress, somewhat like the chorus line in the ballet, all standing in identical costumes, following the same steps of the dance. Each house on its own would have not raised an eyebrow, but put them together and the effect was breathtaking.

Nearing the Assembly Rooms, the traffic began to build. We got stuck in a line of carriages, none of us going anywhere; but this did not prevent some trying, leading to much inventive cursing from the coachmen as the more audacious drivers tried to force their way in front. Two of them started up a fist fight. Imagine it: fighting over something as stupid as bad manners on the road! I thought Bath would be more civilized, but apparently human nature does not change even if the architecture does. I stuck my head out the window to enjoy the show until the duchess pulled me into my seat by the back of my gown and gave me a reproving look.

I'm sorry, Reader, but sometimes my roots can't help getting the better of me.

Some sensible people had resorted to going on foot and were following the flambeaux of link boys as they led the way to the Rooms. I itched to get out and go the last few hundred yards in similar fashion, but no one seconded my suggestion. It appeared that ducal pride would be dented if we did so, which meant we had to sit for an unnecessary quarter of an hour waiting for the blockage to clear.

Finally, it was our turn at the door. Leaving hats and cloaks with the footmen, we entered a packed corridor leading to the rooms beyond. Our names were announced, starting in clarion tones with 'His Grace, the Duke of Avon; Her Grace, the Duchess of Avon; His Lordship, the Earl of Arden; until finally the footman tailed off with 'Mr Dixon, and, um, Miss Royal.' Earl of Arden!? I'd never heard Frank introduced formally before. He'd kept very quiet about his impressive title.

An excited whisper rustled through the people gathered at the sides of the corridor, fans fluttered, spectacles pinched to noses to take a better look. The duke and duchess swept through with gracious nods to acquaintances. Frank offered me his arm with a quizzical smile. I accepted it and we did our best to glide along in their wake, but I would keep tripping on the hem of the duchess's gown.

We were lured onward by the sounds of an orchestra and the clink of glasses. My heart was beating fast with excitement as I took in the beautiful dresses, the glittering mirrors and thousands of candles. Only as I entered the Octagonal Room adjacent to the ballroom did I remember the card on my wrist. It was as blank as when it had first been given to me. Indeed, the flimsy thing hung between us like a manacle, accusing Frank of neglect. He glanced at it once then fixed his eyes on something in the distance. I couldn't remember seeing him look so awkward before. And I sensed it too. It felt as though our friendship was about to move into a whole new territory which neither of us was ready to explore. A step beyond this room and we'd find ourselves in the middle of a dance.

Frank cleared his throat.

'Ah, Arden, you've finally decided to grace us with your presence!' A young man descended on him, a gaggle of ladies in tow. Somehow, with sharp elbows and simpering smiles, they managed to shoulder their way in between us. 'I don't believe you've met my sisters?'

No sooner had these young ladies been introduced than a queue of other female contenders started to form. Matrons thrust me aside as their daughters fought to get to the front. It reminded me of a market crowd getting wind of a bargain, Frank – or should I say the Earl of Arden – being the item on sale. My feet were trodden on and my finery was in grave danger of being ripped in the scrum.

Frank gave me a rueful grin as he was buried under the bevy of giggling girls all wanting to curtsey to the duke's son. I raised my eyebrow in sympathy and turned to seek refuge with the rest of our party. It took a moment to locate them as there were so many people. The room was built for easy passage from refreshment room to ballroom, designed with mingling in mind. Ladies and gentlemen were coming and going the whole time, swirling in their finery around those who had chosen to stand still for a moment. The duke was in earnest conversation with some elderly gentlemen by one of the fireplaces. The duchess had seated herself among four matrons who were all inspecting the finery on display with a critical eye. Mr Dixon was closest. He was greeting a naval officer and a gentleman in a fine purple jacket standing with his back to me. I moved towards them, uncomfortable among all these people who seemed to know each other already.

'Miss Royal, I wondered where you had got to!' Mr Dixon held out his arm and brought me forward. 'May I introduce some acquaintances of mine? Lieutenant Belsize of His Majesty's ship, *Courageous.*' I curtseyed to the young man with ginger hair, resplendent in his dark blue uniform, white breeches and buckled shoes. 'And this gentleman is –'

'Shepherd, Mr William Shepherd – and there is no need for an introduction: Miss Royal and I are old friends.' The man in the purple jacket turned and gave me a grin.

My poise momentarily left me. 'Billy! What the blazes are you doing *here*?'

Mr Dixon and Lieutenant Belsize looked scandalized – as well they might. You don't normally hear language like this from a lady in a ballroom. But perhaps you will forgive me when you understand that Billy and I go all the way back to Covent Garden, beginning our acquaintance – if you can call it that – on the streets. If you have read my earlier adventures, you will know that he has tried to cut my throat twice, but rather spoilt his record by once saving my life.[1] Clawing his way up the social ladder through thieving, threats and thuggery, he now controls one of the most dangerous parts of London and has expanded his interests into legitimate business, no doubt attempting to buy himself respectability. But Bath?

'Language, my dear! Remember where we are,' laughed Billy, taking me by the elbow. I was

---

[1] For throat-cutting attempts, please see *The Diamond of Drury Lane* and *Den of Thieves*; for life-saving, I refer you to *Cat among the Pigeons*, all published by that nice Mr Egmont.

surprised to hear that he had managed to lose much of his street accent, only detectable in his over-aspirated haitches. 'Gentlemen, please excuse us: Miss Royal and I have a lot of catching up to do.'

Still half in shock, I let Billy lead me into the refreshment room. He thrust a glass of punch into my hand.

'At least try and look as though you're enjoying yourself,' he said with a wry smile as he raised his glass.

'Billy, why Bath?' I finally croaked.

'Mr Shepherd to you, my dear.' Billy stroked his magnificent embroidered waistcoat and gazed around the room with satisfaction. 'I'm taking the waters and enjoying the innocent diversions of the place.'

A horrible thought struck me. 'Did you follow me down here?'

'Don't flatter yourself, Cat. That is all at an end.' From the glint in his eye, I could tell we were both thinking back to our last meeting when he had almost killed me for refusing to stay with him as part of his household fixtures and fittings. 'Did you know I'm engaged to be married?'

I spurted a mouthful of punch over him, unable to stop my laughter. 'Who's the victim?' I choked.

He gave me a humourless smile as he wiped himself down with a white silk handkerchief. 'Miss Abingdon, heiress to the Abingdon Brewery fortune.'

'That follows: she'd have to be drunk to marry you.'

'You won't mind, Cat, if I don't introduce you.' Billy's gaze was now roving the company as if looking for someone. 'She's rather a cut above you.'

'Above me? What about you, you lying, thieving, murderous bully! What stone did she find you under?'

He turned back to me, his eyes travelling over my new attire. 'You forget your place, Cat. The dress becomes you well enough, but it doesn't change who you are. One word with the Master of Ceremonies and he'd have you out on the street where you belong, with a flea in your ear for polluting the company. There are few mothers who like their girls mixing with a bastard daughter of some common streetwalker.'

I flushed with rage. He was always trying to drag me down to his level. 'And what if I was to mention to the Master of Ceremonies your little criminal empire?' I spat.

Billy shrugged. 'He'd probably appreciate proof of the depth of my purse. Half the young bloods in Bath are in debt to me.'

'That's not fair.'

'Tell me, Cat: when was your world *ever* fair?' He lifted my chin with his index finger, forcing me to meet his gaze. 'When you got thrown out of the theatre company for being no use to anyone?' His grey-green eyes gleamed maliciously.

You have to hand it to Billy: he certainly knows how to pour salt on a wound.

I had had enough. Rapping his finger away with my fan, I freed myself. 'Well, *Mr* Shepherd, it's been a joy and delight as always to pass the time in your company but I'm afraid I have obligations that tear me from your side.'

I turned to go but a hand shot out and grabbed my arm.

'I believe the next dance is mine,' said Billy.

'You must be joking.' I shook him off. 'Besides, I have a full dance card. I couldn't possibly squeeze you in.'

Billy tugged the card from its ribbon, opened it and laughed. He now brandished it in front of me. 'Come off it, Cat.' His language was sliding back into his old ways. ''Aven't you twigged yet? No one's going to ask you to dance. Look, not even your Lord Francis has demeaned himself to take you out for an 'op. If you don't dance with me, you'll be a wallflower all evenin', common garden variety.'

I bit my lip.

'Aw, I've upset you, Kitten, 'aven't I? But look around you: can't you see the stares you're attractin'? You entered on the arm of the catch of the season so you can bet your last farthin' that all the old dears in the room were quick to smoke you out.' He put down his glass and took mine from my unresisting hand. ''Alf of them are plottin' to snare

Lord Francis so they'll make sure you're no threat to the nice girls. They'll want you ground into the dirt where you belong. I really needn't've threatened to tell the Master of Ceremonies: it's been done already, no doubt. P'rhaps the Avons' influence is enough to protect you from being thrown out on your ear, but I bet all the young men have been warned off approachin' you on pain of disinheritance. As for your little lord, 'e'll make enemies if 'e pays you 'alf a second's notice.' He laughed. 'Such a shame when you're lookin' such a flash mort.'

Humiliated, I knew I was blushing scarlet, never a becoming colour for a redhead like me. How I hated Billy – and the ball with all its fine people who thought themselves too good to breathe the same air as me. I snatched the card back from him, ripped it in half and dropped it in his glass of punch. I just wanted to go home: home to Drury Lane and not back to living as a hanger-on at Boxton, an object of derision to all Frank's circle.

He scanned my face. 'So, Miss Foundling of

Dubious Reputation, does that mean you're going to dance with me or not?' Billy asked in mockingly polite tones, fishing the card out with a smile.

'No.'

'Come, come, don't you want to see me disgrace myself in the ballroom?' He flicked the punch off the card, staining my pretty white dress with droplets. 'Wouldn't that be some recompense – save an otherwise horrible evening?'

He knew me too well. I would relish the chance of getting my own back for his insults. If he thought he could pretend to be a gentleman, let him prove it!

'All right, Billy. Let's see you dance. But don't get angry if I fall about laughing.'

'Nah, Cat, I couldn't get angry with you.' He offered me his hand with a flourish and this time I took it. As we walked into the ballroom, it felt more like we were going to a duel than a dance. The minuet had just finished and the orchestra struck up a cotillion. Good: all the more difficult for Billy to get it right. We moved into position, facing each other, lacking only the pistols to complete the scene.

I curtseyed.

He bowed.

Then the dance began.

Damn and blast him! It took only a few turns for me to realize that he was good – too good. He had an instinctive grace so there was nothing to mock. Dancing as well as elocution lessons – he was doing the gentleman thing properly. He grinned at me when he saw I had noticed his faultless steps. We came together for a hand spin.

'Really, Cat, you must say something, you know; it's only polite,' he commented as we passed.

I wanted to ask him why he always had to turn up and spoil things for me, but he'd only take that as proof he was winning.

'If you want polite, then I hope you and Miss Abingdon will be very happy together,' I said sweetly.

'Hah!' he gave a derisive snort. 'Actually, I don't come to you for polite. Miss Abingdon is an ugly old stick well past her prime. I doubt we'll see much of each other after we're wed.'

'Then why marry you?'

'My beloved's business owes me a lot of money; in fact, everyone seems to owe me a lot of money these days. It's why I can afford to dance with you.'

I ignored the dig with Olympian calm. 'Well, I must say, you dance well for a vicious cut-throat. All that running from the Bow Street runners must've done you good.'

'Yes, we've both had a lot of practice at that. I think we make a charming couple.'

The dance came to an end and he bowed to kiss my hand. Thank goodness I was wearing a glove. Time to end this charade. I turned abruptly on my heel, whipped my hand out of reach, and left him kissing the air.

I had reached the corridor to the cloakroom when I felt a hand on my shoulder. Billy was breathing down my neck, far too close.

'Miss Royal, we're not through yet. Perhaps you are not accustomed to ballroom etiquette? You owe me a pair, a second dance, that's the rule.'

'I owe you nothing, Billy.'

Our altercation was attracting the stares of the footmen on duty. Billy backed me into an alcove behind a potted palm.

'I've offended you, 'aven't I, Cat? You don't like it that I'm risin' above you. You never thought I'd cut it as a gentleman.' His face was a study in self-satisfaction.

'Rising above me? Don't fool yourself.'

He leant closer, his face serious now. 'But I'm glad you're 'ere, Kitten. I've been wantin' to make you an offer.'

'You've nothing to offer that I could possibly want.' I took a step back, not liking what I saw in his expression.

'No?'

With snakelike swiftness, he darted forward and clamped his mouth on mine. His kiss was hot and fierce. I was too stunned to do anything – I couldn't even break away as his arm circled my waist, crushing me to him. My heart was racing, my legs turning to water.

Then it got worse.

'You said she went this way?' said Frank as he and Mr Dixon walked in upon us. 'Cat!'

Billy looked up and relaxed his hold enough for me to push him away. I fled, his laughter ringing in my ears.

'Lord Francis, how delightful to see you again,' Billy crowed, his voice following me down the corridor, 'but I'm afraid your timing leaves a lot to be desired.'

Mortified, I hid for the next hour in the ladies' cloakroom until the stares of the attendant became too hostile for me to ignore. I moved then to the hat room by the front door, talking my way in thanks to the friendly black footman who had heard of Pedro. I helped out by handing him the hats as the gentlemen presented their tickets at the window.

'You shouldn't be doing that, miss,' my new friend said. 'You should be enjoying yourself.'

'But I am enjoying myself, Sam – here with you. I shouldn't have tried mixing with the likes of them.' I jerked my head towards the ballroom where the music was still playing.

'Number six hundred and sixty-six,' a familiar voice announced at the window, handing over a ticket. I tried to duck down behind a naval officer's bicorne but Billy had spotted me. 'So that's where my blushing partner ran off to.' I wordlessly passed a black silk hat to Sam, who in turn handed it to Shepherd. Billy tipped it to me as he put it on his head. 'A most amusing evening. I'll be seeing you soon, Miss Royal. We need to finish our interrupted conversation.' And he left.

'Who was that?' asked Sam, pocketing the generous tip Billy had left him.

'A low-down, conniving, vicious, son of a –'

Perhaps it was fortunate for the innocent Sam that I was unable to continue.

Hot on Billy's trail, Frank appeared at the window. He glanced out of the door in time to see him climbing into his carriage, then looked back at me.

'Cat, is this where you've been all evening? I've been looking everywhere for you. What are you doing here? Were you and he . . .?' He gestured towards the coach.

'No, we were not,' I said tartly, getting up to depart. 'Sam, thank you for the refuge.'

'Any time, miss. Send my best wishes to Pedro. Tell him he did us all proud last year.'

'I will.' And with that I thrust Frank's hat into his arms and marched out to the Avon carriage.

To say that the atmosphere in the carriage was Arctic would be an understatement. The North Pole is positively warm compared to the rear-facing seat that night. The duke and duchess chatted merrily about their acquaintances, oblivious to the awkwardness opposite them. I was desperate to be home, get out of my ridiculous outfit and put the evening behind me. The very worst of it all was the nagging realization that part of me – a very small rebellious part, it must be said – had been excited by the kiss. My first proper kiss. Syd had once pecked me on the lips but that had not really counted. Of course, I was revolted by Billy – he was more toad than prince – but the kiss felt somehow . . . dangerous.

Perhaps I should stop being so candid, Reader. You will probably be thinking all sorts of terrible things about me now I've admitted this much. But I've never liked the safe or the conventional. And it's not that I'm in love with Billy or anything – grant me some taste, please! But the experience had been – how can I put it? – illuminating.

On arrival at Boxton near midnight, Frank foiled my attempt to slink off unchallenged. He took my arm.

'I want a word with you.'

Mr Dixon passed us in the hall, casting an odd look at me. I felt my cheeks flush again, knowing I had shattered any hope I had had that I could persuade him that I was a proper lady, worthy of Frank's friendship and trust.

'It's late, Frank. Can't it wait?' I replied wearily.

'No, it can't, Catherine Royal.'

Escorting me into the library, Frank sat me down in a chair. He paced in front of the fire for a moment.

'So, what have you got to say for yourself?' he

managed at last, sounding like some pompous father from a Fanny Burney novel.

'Me? Say? Nothing. It was you who wanted to talk to me, remember, Frank?'

'I hope you realize you've disgraced yourself – and my family – by kissing that man like that in public.'

I felt a surge of anger. 'Look, my lord, it was *him* kissing *me*!'

'Well, it looked to me as if you were both enjoying yourselves.'

'Frank!'

'I don't understand you, Cat. I thought you hated him.'

'I do, but – '

Frank waved his hand dismissively. 'It doesn't matter. I just want you to understand that kissing is not appropriate behaviour for a lady.'

How dare he preach to me!

'I don't know if you've noticed, Frank, but I'm not a lady. I'm a foundling of dubious reputation, apparently. Didn't you see how everyone snubbed me? Billy was the only person who came near me all evening. The rest of you were a load of arrogant prigs with pokers up the –'

'Now don't change the subject, Cat.'

'I'm not changing the subject; I'm trying to tell you what happened. You all think you're too good for the likes of me, and perhaps you are.' Oh Lord, he was the Earl of Arden for heaven's sake. He really was above me. I swallowed a sob and ploughed on. 'But at least Billy, for whatever twisted reason of his own, deigned to ask me to dance. Even you – one of my best friends – couldn't humble yourself to do that, could you?'

'What?' Frank was confused that his accusation of me had somehow returned as criticism of him. 'I didn't . . . you can't think I failed to ask you to dance because I don't respect you?'

'Well, *do* you respect me?'

'Yes, of course!'

'I don't believe you. You've already said you were ashamed of me. Anyway, Lord Francis, yes, I admit that I danced with Billy Shepherd, but only because I wanted him to look stupid. But, do you know something? He didn't. He did us street people credit. Then he followed me out of the ballroom and . . . and kissed me.' I paused, remembering rather too vividly the sensation of Billy's lips on mine. Frank looked so horrified that I felt an urge to punish him for his prudishness. 'In fact, you are right: I quite liked it. And now I'm off to bed, if you don't mind. No need to fret about the family honour because I'm packing my bags and heading back to London. I won't be around to embarrass you with my vulgar ways any longer.'

And then I flounced from the room, something my new gown allowed me to do very well, leaving Frank gaping by the fire.

You may be assured, Reader, that I had the decency, when preparing for bed, to take myself to task. It was a low trick to turn my behaviour into Frank's fault. And, I know, I know, dangerous is bad. All the novels I've ever read tell me that – just look at Clarissa and Lovelace, Pamela and Mr B, Joseph Andrews and Lady Booby. One slightly enjoyable kiss does not change the fact that Billy Shepherd kills, terrorizes and exploits people for a living.

It was only when I had blown out my candle that it struck me that my wish had come true: I had met the man of my dreams at the ball. Unfortunately, no one had warned me that he would be the stuff of nightmares.

SCENE 2 – PRESS GANG

I did not feel brave enough to face Frank at breakfast so I took an early walk in the shrubbery. Not a good idea in December as everything was damp and cold. Sandy paths snaked through dark avenues of yew, netted with dewy spider's webs. From time to time, I caught a glimpse of Boxton House at the end of a hedge-corridor, framed like some magnificent palace painted by our set designer, De Loutherbourg, on a backdrop at Drury Lane, the lines of yew giving the *trompe l'oeil* illusion of depth. Only here, of course, in Frank's world, the fairy palace was real and not a canvas that could be rolled up and put in store. I retreated into a dank summer house to shiver and indulge my fit of melancholy homesickness.

'Cat?' It was Pedro. He was searching the garden for me. I stepped out on to the path and waved to him. 'What on earth are you doing in this dismal place?' he asked as he approached.

'Being dismal, of course.'

'So I take it last night wasn't a success?'

'I wouldn't say it was totally wasted – I met one of your admirers. He sends his regards.'

'Oh?' Pedro glowed with pleasure. 'Who was that?'

'Sam Otoba.'

'An African brother? Where did you meet him?'

'In the hat room.' I plucked a berry from a spray of holly and flicked it on to the ground.

Pedro turned me to look at him. 'And what were you doing in there?'

I cracked. 'Oh, Pedro, it was awful. Everyone knew where I came from and none of them wanted anything to do with me. The only person who talked to me was Billy Shepherd –'

'Shepherd? What was he doing there?'

'Lord knows. Anyway, it all went horribly wrong when he kissed me –'

'He what?'

'And Frank walked in upon us. He thinks I . . . well, I'm not sure what he thinks, but it's not good.'

'Oh, Cat, you silly goose!'

'Now, don't you start, Pedro! I couldn't bear it. Anyway, I've said I'll go back to London.'

'But you've nowhere to go!'

I brushed aside this technicality: the dramatic gesture seemed fitting. 'I can't face Frank and Mr Dixon again.'

'What's Dixon got to do with it?'

'He saw it all too.'

Pedro smiled.

'Don't – this is serious!'

'What? A stolen kiss? Hardly.'

'It is – I'm a disgrace, according to Frank.'

Pedro put his arm around my shoulders. 'Look, Frank is a fine person in many respects but we both know he can be a fool. He was probably just jealous.'

'Jealous!' This was getting worse and worse.

'Oh, Cat, you're always so hard on yourself. You're funny, brave, pretty – of course Shepherd wanted to kiss you: he'd be a fool not to take the chance. It's nothing.' He waved it away with an elegant gesture.

I sighed, feeling the weight begin to drop from

my shoulders by Pedro's practical attitude to the matter. I straightened up. He was right: I hadn't done anything unforgivable. I'd just been caught unprepared, out of my depth.

'Thanks, Pedro. You're a good friend.'

'Ready to face Frank then?'

I shook my head.

'Well, you'd better be – because he's coming this way.'

It was too late to bolt. Frank was striding towards us with a determined look.

'Pedro, would you mind? I'd like to talk to Cat alone for a moment,' he said sternly.

What did this mean? Was the carriage already at the door?

'Of course. I'll see you in the breakfast room.' Pedro grinned and scooted off into the house. The traitor.

'Cat, I just wanted to say –' continued Frank.

'You don't have to say anything.' My misery was complete: I was to be dismissed in disgrace. 'I'm sorry about last night. It wasn't what it seemed – it never is with Billy. As for leaving, it really is time I returned to my real life and stopped pretending to be a fine lady when we all know I'm –'

Frank put his hand over my mouth. 'Don't you ever shut up for a moment?'

'Hmm-hmm-hmm.' But my reply was lost.

'Before I was rudely interrupted, I was trying to apologize to you. I over-reacted and I neglected you. You had a horrible evening and that was my fault. As for you marching off to London, I won't hear of it. You're my friend and we're going to stick together for as long as possible.'

'Hmm-hmm . . .!' (By which I meant 'But Frank – !')

'No "buts", Cat. I'm off to college next year: we don't have long to turn you into a proper horsewoman. We'd better get to work!' He took his hand away.

'But – !'

He swiftly replaced it. 'I said "no buts" and I mean it. I don't care if all the stupid people in Bath think you're beneath them: I know you're first rate and I'm always proud of you, any time, in any company. And I would've been honoured to dance with you if I could've plucked up the courage to ask.'

He took his hand away again but I was speechless.

'That's better. Now, breakfast.' Frank offered me his arm and escorted me back into the house.

Joseph returned from Bristol having drawn a blank. No one had seen or heard anything of Syd – or so they said. I was beginning to get anxious.

'You know who we should ask, don't you?' I said to Frank as he trotted beside me on his black gelding, Amigo. My mount, Beauty, was a docile grey mare, just right for incompetents like me. We were riding through the beautiful parkland that surrounded Boxton. It was still hard to believe that it would one day all belong to my friend. A herd of deer scattered on our approach, bounding into a leafless copse and vanishing among the grey trunks. It should've been an idyllic scene except I was in continual fear of falling. I think I would have taken more to riding if I hadn't had to perch side-saddle. I always felt in imminent danger of sliding off – and had done so on more than one occasion.

'No, who should we talk to?' asked Frank, tapping Beauty back into line with his crop.

'Billy Shepherd. He always knows things. Syd's his enemy – you can bet he keeps an eye on him just out of habit if nothing else.'

Frank groaned.

'I know how you feel,' I said. I had been in debt to Billy before and didn't want to repeat the experience.

'Do you know where he's lodging?' asked Frank.

I shook my head.

'It can't be difficult to discover,' Frank continued, taking a swipe at the dried stalks of cow parsley in the hedge, probably imagining them as Billy's head. 'I'll ride over and talk to him.'

'Not a good idea. I suggest we catch him unawares – somewhere public. It'll give him less chance to exploit the situation.'

'We?' Frank tipped his hat back with the top of his whip. 'So anxious to see him again?'

I wasn't in the mood for teasing. 'No, I'm just

anxious to help Syd. Billy tells me things, you know that. He said he was here to take the waters; if that's true, then we should be able to surprise him in the Pump Room.'

'Well, the fashionable time to drink the waters is before ten,' sighed Frank. 'Looks like an early start tomorrow.'

Mr Dixon accompanied us to the Pump Room, saying he had business to conduct in town. I rather wished he had decided to stay behind as I couldn't help but feel awkward with him in the carriage. Neither of us had mentioned Monday night – he was too much of a gentleman to allude to it, of course, but he must be wondering about me. His charming demeanour had become cold and somewhat strained when I was around. I was, therefore, pleased to lose him in the crowd when we entered the Pump Room.

'I suppose now I'm here I should try the stuff,' I remarked to Frank, wrinkling my nose over the evil-smelling glass the footman had offered me from the ornate fountain. We were in a large, light room with a high ceiling. An orchestra played at one end while the visitors circulated, greeting each other. It was like watching a selection of fashion plates parade before you, each dress, jacket and uniform chosen to impress. There was something forced about it all, the preening and strutting too self-consciously done. Not having much to strut and preen about, I preferred to turn to the real business of the Pump Room: that of taking the water. I'd heard it was wonderfully good for you.

'Rather you than me,' Frank replied. I should have been warned by his amused expression.

'Well, down the hatch.' I took a sip and retched as a sulphurous taste attacked my throat. 'Ugh! That is disgusting!'

'I thought I recognized those dulcet tones!' Billy Shepherd separated himself from the crowd and thumped me on the back as I coughed and spluttered. It had worked: my presence had been bait enough. I suppose I should have been flattered. Frank stiffened but pretended to be uninterested in the new arrival.

'I hope you're not sickening for something,

Miss Royal?' Billy asked with mock concern, as I stood up, eyes streaming.

'Just trying to remove an unpleasant taste left behind from Monday,' I said hoarsely, wiping my mouth on a handkerchief.

'Really?' Billy's eyes were fixed on my lips. 'I was left with a most pleasant sensation – a powerful tingle right here.' He touched his mouth. 'I could've sworn it was mutual.'

I could feel the blush rushing up my neck. 'That shows how much you know about me.'

'Doesn't it just?' There was a pause that I rather wished someone would fill, before Billy offered me his arm. 'As the Earl of Arden will no doubt tell you, the done thing is to circulate.'

I hesitated, then took the offered arm. As loath as I was to touch him again, there seemed little choice if we were to talk. With Frank on one side and Billy on the other, we began to move through the crowds. I was used to everyone making a point of greeting Frank but I was surprised to note the number of people who nodded respectfully to Billy. He saw me watching and, leaning down, began to mutter under his breath for my entertainment:

'In debt for a hundred. That one . . . let me see . . . I think it's only fifty pounds – a trifle. I'm surprised he bothers to nod. Now that one – blown everything on a very disreputable woman who lodges in Gay Street – in debt to the tune of a thousand. Interest racking up daily.' We passed Mr Dixon talking to an unfamiliar lady. 'You'll be curious about that one – mortgaged to the hilt. I own everything now.'

'What, the lady?'

'No, the gent.'

I glanced up at Frank to see if he had heard but he was chewing his lip with a distracted expression as a line of girls curtseyed to him. He was doubtless wondering what everyone thought seeing a duke's son in this questionable company.

'Cousin of your friend, isn't he?' continued Billy in a low voice. 'I'm squeezin' pretty 'ard – he might go under if he don't cough up soon. Such a shame my lord is so hale and hearty. All Mr D's money troubles would be solved if his cousin croaked – next in line, you see?'

'You wouldn't . . .!' It was no joke to hear Billy make reflections on Frank's longevity. I glanced fearfully over at him.

'Nah, don't worry, Cat.' Billy stroked my arm as if soothing my bristled fur. 'I'm not after 'im, though as 'is friend you should keep your eyes peeled – there's bound to be others who are.'

'Who?' I cast an anxious look round the room, half-expecting to see cloaked assassins behind every potted palm.

'Scheming mothers mostly.' Billy chuckled. 'Not life-threatening – but pretty dangerous to health and happiness. The Marchioness of Westbury was devastated that he didn't ask her girl for a dance at the ball; same with the Countess of Gunnersford. These noble mothers are spoiling for revenge because the gossip is he wasted half the dances looking for you, desperate to save you from the clutches of your devilish admirer. You are quite the talk of the town.' Billy gave me a wink. 'Not that you needed rescuing. That kiss was long overdue and it's only the start, but perhaps that's a discussion we should have on our own somewhere less public.'

Billy Shepherd truly has a gift for disconcerting me. I did not know where to start with my denials. 'Billy, I –'

'And then, of course, there are the jilted suitors,' continued Billy, squeezing my hand. 'None of the other young men are getting a look in with the heiresses while the ladies have their hopes pinned on catching the Earl of Arden. Quite a few of the gents are muttering darkly that life was much better before he arrived.'

Frank turned his attention back to us. 'What's that you're saying? Who's arrived?'

'Nothing,' I said quickly.

'We were just discussing your marital prospects,' slipped in Billy.

Frank went red. 'I'll ask you to keep your nose out of –'

'Frank!' I exclaimed. Had he forgotten that we were trying to wheedle information out of Shepherd, not start a punch-up?

Billy came to a halt. 'So, Cat, why is my lord here lowering himself to spend time in my company? And you – I thought you never wanted to see me again?'

'Well, you know I can't resist your witty repartee and faultless manners,' I said with a simper that I knew would annoy him.

'Cut it out, Cat. You want somethink.'

'And what if we do?'

'You know nothing comes cheap with me.' His expression was unpleasantly suggestive.

'Well, I think I made a payment on account on Monday – you certainly took without asking. You owe me.'

He scratched his chin, running one finger over his lips. 'Perhaps I do. Go on, then, spit it out.'

'It's about Syd.'

'Ah. You don't know then?'

'Know what?'

Billy threw his head back and roared with laughter.

I fumed silently.

'I love it when you get all worked up, Cat,' he said at last. 'And I can see I'm annoying you now.'

Frank stepped in between us. 'Stop taunting her, Shepherd. If you claim to be a gentleman, start acting like one.'

'Ooh, got you angry too, have I?' Shepherd grinned and began to walk away.

Frank made a move to follow but I grabbed his arm. 'Wait,' I cautioned.

Billy turned when he realized we weren't pursuing him. His eyes locked on mine, gleaming with amusement. 'Go to the docks at Bristol. Ask at the *Honest Tar*.'

'Is this a trick, Billy?'

'Would I trick you, Cat Royal?'

'Yes.'

'For once, I'm trying to do you a favour. The kiss was worth it.'

'The *Honest Tar*?' Mr Dixon rubbed the bridge of his nose thoughtfully as the carriage rumbled back to Boxton. We had left the honey-coloured stone houses of Bath behind and returned to the landscape of thatched cottages and farms of the estate. 'That's not good. A rough place by all accounts. I really don't like the idea of you exposing yourself to danger, Frank.'

'Well, we've no choice. We've got to find out

what's happened to Syd,' I said, staring out of the window miserably. Talking with Billy always did this to me: there was a temporary exhilaration of crossing swords with him, matching my wit against his, followed by the depressing awareness of my own fallibility. I realized I was missing Syd. He never made me feel cheap and he always treated me with respect.

'Well, if we must go, then I suggest we go in force,' replied Mr Dixon, giving me an encouraging smile. 'We should dress so as not to attract attention and take a footman for our protection. That Joseph fellow should do: he's big enough.'

'You're coming with us?' I asked, impressed by his demonstration of bravery in a matter that did not concern him.

'Of course.' Mr Dixon patted my hand. 'I can't leave a friend of my cousin in distress, can I? Frank and I have been in many a scrape together before.'

'Hang on a minute, Cat.' Frank now entered the conversation, ready for battle. 'You can't seriously expect us to take you with us!'

'Why not?' I knew this was coming and had my armoury of arguments ready.

'It's too dangerous.'

'Let me ask you a question, my lord: who's been living in luxury since he was born and who's been looking after herself on the streets since she could walk?'

'That's not the point, Cat.'

'Isn't it?'

'Will, talk to her, please!'

'To be honest with you, Frank,' said Mr Dixon, shaking out the newspaper he'd taken from his pocket, 'I cannot see that having a young lady as one of the party will put any of us at risk, rather the opposite. People will assume we're just out for a night on the town. Miss Royal will doubtless rise above any reflections on her character that may result. I think she is used to doing that. *Honi soit qui mal y pense.*[2]'

What a wonderful man! I gave Mr Dixon a beaming smile.

[2] Shame on him who thinks evil.

'Thank you, sir. I care little for false propriety when my friends are in danger.' I wanted to add that I was sure Frank and his family would stand by him in his monetary difficulties with Billy, but knew I must hold my tongue. I wasn't supposed to know and he would not thank me for broadcasting it.

Mr Dixon returned my smile. 'Quite so. Then that's settled.'

With hindsight, I should have listened to Frank, not Mr Dixon. Instead, I found myself entering the *Honest Tar* at nine that evening in the company of Frank, Pedro, Mr Dixon and Joseph. It was a low place, somewhat like the *Jolly Boatman* back home off The Strand: the only attraction the cheap beer dispensed by a rouged barmaid. Frank bought a round for everyone and carried our drinks to the table.

'What now?' he asked, slopping the beer on to the unwashed surface.

'Get talking to people,' I whispered, pushing my mug away. I didn't like beer as it made my head swim and I knew I had to stay alert. 'I'll talk to the maid – you know, woman to woman. I'll tell her Syd's my long-lost sweetheart, see if I can get her on my side.' (This wasn't so very far from the truth.)

Pedro got up. 'I'll tackle those sailors over there.' He took out his violin, which he'd had the foresight to bring. 'Come on, Frank.'

'And I'll see what headway I can make with some of the regulars,' Mr Dixon volunteered gamely. 'Be careful, everyone.'

We all went our separate ways. It wasn't long before the inn began to fill with merry tunes courtesy of Pedro's fiddle – a bit of a comedown from Handel, but he wasn't too proud to help Syd with a few sea-shanties. I sidled over to the barmaid.

'Lovely,' she sighed, her blonde curls jiggling as she tapped her foot. 'A friend of yours?' She nodded to Pedro.

'Yes.'

She flicked a cloth at a fly settled on the remnants of a customer's supper. 'What brings you to Bristol, my duck?'

Good – she was a curious one: that boded well for my enquiries.

'We're looking for a friend of ours.' I leant closer. 'My fiancé.'

She clucked her tongue sympathetically. 'Men! You can't trust them. Promise you the moon, then sling their hook.'

'Not Syd. He wouldn't leave me without a word. I'm afraid something's happened to him.'

She smiled sceptically and continued to wipe the mugs with her cloth.

'You might've seen him,' I continued.

'I see a lot of men, my duck.'

'But Syd's special.'

'You poor thing.' She patted my cheek. 'Best if you forget him. A pretty thing like you won't have to wait long for someone to take his place.'

'No, I'm telling the truth! Syd's not like that. Look, he's big – about six foot – blonde, handsome. Nose been broken. A boxer.'

Her eyes lit up. 'A boxer, you say?'

'Yes. He might've been with another man, a sharp dresser with a face like a fox.'

She put her cloth down. 'I know the very ones! They were in here not so long ago celebrating a victory over a seaman, the ship's champion. Not very clever of them: they should've taken their party away from the tars.'

'What happened to him?' I asked eagerly.

'Nothing – well, not in here at any rate.'

'Go on.'

The maid pursed her lips. 'I'm not saying nothing, mind, but the *Courageous* is trying to fill its quota. It lost half its men to yellow fever last voyage. And no one wants to serve with Captain Barton, of course.'

'You mean the press gang got him?'

'As I said, I'm not saying nothing.' She picked up her cloth again and wiped a few tankards dry. She paused. 'Word is the *Courageous* sails on the tide. You'd better hurry. I hope he's worth it.'

I darted back to Frank in a panic.

'The barmaid as good as told me Syd's on the *Courageous*. We've got to be quick – it's ready to sail!'

Frank gave a nod to Joseph, who'd been standing guard by the door, then turned to find his cousin. Mr Dixon was sharing a pint with a surly-looking man in a corner. On seeing us rise to leave, he shook hands with his companion and followed us out.

The sailors, however, were not so eager to lose Pedro.

'Just one more, boy!' they pleaded, work-calloused hands stretched out in appeal.

'Later!' Pedro laughed, packing his violin away.

We headed towards the waterfront, shouldering our way through the parties of seamen on shore leave. I stuck close to Joseph, not wishing to attract any unwelcome attention.

'Any idea where the *Courageous* is tied up?' Frank asked his cousin.

Mr Dixon was clearly feeling no more at ease than I. He kept looking nervously over his shoulder. 'I think it put in for repairs so it'll be in the shipyard. Down here, if my memory serves me well.' He pointed to a dark alley, a filthy gutter running down the middle of the cobbles. Not good.

'Isn't there another way?' I asked, catching his sleeve.

'Probably, but I don't know it if there is.' He took my hand and guided me around a black puddle. 'Do not fear, Miss Royal, we will protect you.'

I tried to put my faith in his chivalrous attention, but I knew something was wrong as soon as we left the main thoroughfare. My city-bred instincts were screaming that this was a bad idea.

'Let's go back.' I made to pull away but my gallant defender had my arm linked through his. Joseph hovered at my shoulder, waiting for the command to retreat. Frank and Pedro hesitated behind him.

'We're almost there,' Mr Dixon said, tugging me forward resolutely. 'Courage, Miss Royal, courage!'

As I stumbled on, a group of men appeared out of the shadows in front of us. Footsteps approached at speed from behind. Joseph cursed and took up a defensive stance at the rear; Frank moved to my unprotected side, Pedro beside him.

'Run!' I shouted. It was our best chance of escape.

Mr Dixon started forward, throwing himself between me and the cudgel-wielding thug in front of us, but was knocked back into a doorway. I rushed to help him, but he slumped to the ground, clutching his stomach. Then he raised his hands to me – they were covered in blood. I screamed as someone wrenched me away, breaking Mr Dixon's grip on my skirt. My upbringing took over. A kick to the shins – and to somewhere else – and my surprised assailant grunted, falling back against the brick wall. I glanced about me to find out what had happened to the rest of my party. Joseph was out cold, sprawled on the ground as two bullies grappled with Frank. Pedro was fighting like a tiger with a bow-legged Chinaman, using his violin case to hit the man over the head. I charged into the biggest of Frank's attackers, only to bounce off the mountain of muscle.

'Go, Cat!' shouted Frank, head caught in an armlock. 'Get help!'

I picked myself up and made a dash for the end of the alleyway, dodging past two men, before running smack into the fist of a third.

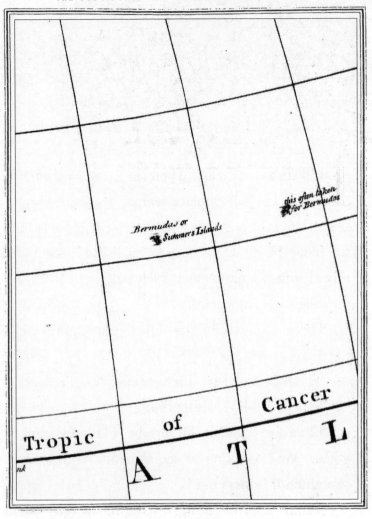

*Act II — In which Cat finds
herself marked for life...*

ACT II

SCENE 1 – COURAGEOUS

I came to with my head in someone's lap. It was still dark – at least, wherever I lay was pitch black. The whole place seemed to be swaying, but that might only have been the after-effects of the blow. There was a strange smell in the air: tar mixed with stagnant water. I felt sick.

'She's coming round!'

There was scuffling around me and someone put a cup to my lips.

'Try and drink this.' I recognized Pedro's voice.

'Where am I?' I whispered.

'On a ship,' said Pedro tersely. 'The press gang got us. We're waiting to see someone so we can straighten this mess out.'

'What they're doing bringing a girl on board, I don't know!' That was Frank. 'But don't worry: Joseph or Will must've raised the alarm by now.'

'How long have I been out?' My memory was slowly returning.

'Hours. You took a nasty blow to the head,' explained Pedro.

'Is it me, or are we at sea?'

Pedro sighed. 'They set sail immediately after we were thrown aboard. It's common to keep press-ganged men below until there's no hope of escape. We expect they'll come and check on us soon and discover their mistake.'

'Are you both all right?' I asked. I felt my face gingerly in the dark: my left eye was closed by swelling. I must have one ugly black eye.

'A few bruises, that's all,' said Frank. He reached out and stroked my hair. 'You had us worried there, Cat.'

Suddenly, it all came back. 'But Mr Dixon! He was covered in blood — stabbed in the stomach.'

'What?' Frank exclaimed in horror.

'Yes, he collapsed in a doorway. I tried to reach him but they pulled me away.'

Frank gave an agonized groan. 'This is all my

fault: I should never've let him come – nor you!'

I tried to sit up, but I was feeling wretched. My head ached as if it had been split in two. 'But they can't keep us here: you're a peer of the realm. And as for me, I'm obviously not fit material for the crew.'

'You're right. We've got to get back to Bristol at once and find Will. Dear God, I hope he's not too badly injured!' Frank beat his fist on the planks of the bulkhead in anger. 'Someone's going to pay for this!'

I didn't want to say any more to Frank, but from the amount of blood I'd seen, it looked to me like a serious wound. Few men recover from belly cuts, and death was usually slow and painful. Yes, we had to get back to him as soon as possible.

But nobody came. Hours passed. I fell into a fitful doze, seasickness fighting to gain the upper hand of misery from my headache. Pedro and Frank looked after me as best they could, but they were suffering too. When I touched Pedro, I could feel him shaking. I was afraid that being locked up in this dark hold had brought back bad memories of his time aboard a slave ship. Frank could hardly contain his rage: he was not used to being treated like this. Duke's sons don't as a rule get press-ganged like common folk.

As I lay there, listening to the creaking of the timbers and slosh of water not far below, I tried to piece together what had happened. I couldn't understand why they had taken me, obviously no able-bodied landsman. And why leave Joseph if they were after men? Had he been badly injured too? And Frank, so clearly a gentleman, not press gang fodder. None of it made sense.

A rattling at the door announced that we were about to get some answers. As it creaked open, we were dazzled by the light of a lantern. The door slammed shut again and a man stumped forward, holding the light up to each of us in turn.

'Still alive then, eh?' he grunted.

Frank stood up, crackling with anger. 'Now just what do you think you're doing holding us down here? I'm the Earl of Arden, son of the Duke of Avon. You made a big mistake when you laid hands on me!'

The man just chuckled. He had a cruel face marked by a shiny burn running down his cheek to his neck.

'And as for taking this lady on board: you've got some explaining to do to your captain.'

'I see no lady,' growled the seaman. 'I just see three new recruits for the *Courageous*. Welcome aboard, shipmates.'

'Is this a joke?' I asked, struggling to my feet and pointedly shaking out my skirts. 'If so I find it in very poor taste.'

'I demand to see the captain,' declared Frank.

'Nah, you don't,' said the man.

'You can't stop me!'

'Can too.' The sailor sat down on a barrel and threw a bundle on the planks in front of us. 'You don't get it, do you?'

'Get what?' Frank seethed.

'Haven't you heard? Your girl here is wanted for the attempted murder of a Mr William Dixon. She's also thought to have done away with that duke's son you mentioned; at any rate, he's feared lost, dumped in the river, most like.'

'M-me? I'm supposed to have done this?' I stammered.

The sailor held up the lamp to my dress. 'See? The evidence's all over her.'

I looked down. You could make out the bloody hand print where Mr Dixon had clasped my skirt.

'But that's preposterous!' exclaimed Frank. '*I'm* the Duke of Avon's son; Cat had nothing to do with the attack on Mr Dixon – that was the press gang.'

'The press gang don't go laying unlawful hands on young lords. No, that was her and her accomplices, or so the Bristol magistrate thinks. He's moving heaven and earth to capture her. The papers will be full of it by now – how his lordship's cousin used his last words to gasp her name before he passed out from his injuries.'

I couldn't believe it. How could anyone think I'd do such a thing to one of my best friends? With a horrid sinking feeling, I then realized that it was all too likely. How often had I been told by Billy that few people believed my friendship with the Avons to be genuine? Perhaps they were all waiting for something like this to happen?

Pedro stepped forward to face our captor. 'What do you want? Money? How much?'

'Ah, at least one of you has your wits about you,' nodded the sailor. 'Quicker off the mark than these two, ain't you, slave boy? But don't you worry, I'm already well paid for my trouble. Get the young lord out of the country, that's what I was told. Not a knife in the ribs then? Nah, he's too squeamish for that. Get him away and keep him quiet, he says. People will all too easily think the worst of his low friends and blame them. Then let nature take its course. It's a dangerous life at sea.' Our tormentor sat back, clearly pleased with this last speech.

'But I won't keep quiet,' snarled Frank. 'Not after this treatment!'

'Aye, you will. Or else I hand her over to Captain Barton.' The man jerked his head at me.

'So?' Frank tilted his head back, in bearing every inch the lord.

'Not heard of Captain Barton, lad? Barmy Barton, we call him, but not to his face. Not a kind man, our captain: rumour has it he's pursued by demons from his past; they drive him fair mad. Makes him angry too. Finds a fugitive on board, wanted for murder, and what you think he'll do? He'll not bother to lose time and go back to a British port. No, it'll be a summary judgement and execution; it's his ship: he has the power and he likes using it. Ask the hands who saw him hang those men at Gibraltar. Best day of his life, he said.'

I shuddered.

'I'll tell him who I am, prove she is innocent. You can't expect to get away with this,' said Frank, putting his arm protectively round my shoulders.

'Aye, that I do. Look at the state of you – no one will believe you are a lord.' It was true: Frank's clothes were ripped and filthy from the fight. 'They'll think you're in it with her, fleeing the scene of the crime. And you'd not risk letting them think otherwise – for if I see so much as one of you lads sniffing around the officers, bleating your story, then she'll suffer. Just think how easy it'll be for me to snuff out a little life like hers; there are knives and ropes aplenty. Or maybe she'll just disappear one dark night. Splash over the side and goodbye.'

I was beginning to feel panic-stricken. He wasn't intending to keep me here awaiting my death, locked up in the dark throughout the long months of the voyage, was he? I'd go mad.

'I beg you, sir, don't leave me down here. Let me be with my friends,' I choked out.

'Aw, a sweet little thing, isn't she?' said the sailor, turning to Frank and Pedro, both of whom were looking sick with fear. 'Worth protecting, don't you think? Now don't you fret, lass, that's all thought of. You can't stay here.'

'Then let me go; put me ashore somewhere before I'm discovered!'

'Nah, no need. I've been told you're no lady, for all your fine clothes. "She's a nobody," he said. "Got way above her station."'

I was trembling with terror and rage.

'Who's this man you speak of?' I spat. 'It's that sewer rat Shepherd, isn't it? He paid you to do this?'

Frank squeezed my shoulders in warning. 'It might not be him,' he murmured.

The tirade died on my tongue. Frank was right. I was used to thinking of Shepherd as the enemy but why would he bother to keep us alive? Yet if it wasn't him, then who? The person who stood most to gain from getting Frank out the way was Mr Dixon. But he was like a brother and, anyway, why plot an attack in which you get yourself murdered? It made no sense. That left jealous suitors and vengeful mothers. Frank had made himself a number of enemies of late – any one of them could be behind this outrage.

The sailor leant forward conspiratorially, snagging a fistful of my straggling hair to pull me towards him. 'Your well-wisher said he wants you taught a lesson and I have the very thing. Do you want to hear it?'

I shook my head mutely.

'You're going to hear it, like it or not. I was told you like dressing up when the fancy takes you, think it rare sport. As it happens, I need a new cabin boy since the last one died of fever. So get changed. You too, lads.' He kicked the bundle towards us. Pedro knelt down to open it: it had three sets of sailors' clothes: loose trousers, short jackets and caps.

I'd had more than my fill of pretending to be a boy at Frank's school.

'I can't! I won't!' I protested.

My answer was a blow from the back of his hand that sent me reeling. I fell to the floor, my lip bleeding. Frank started forward to strike back, but Pedro caught him by the jacket.

'That's right, son, keep him quiet,' the sailor laughed softly. 'I see you understand. Any more of that and it'll be the worse for her. She's the purser's boy from now onwards, somewhat prone to wild imaginings but no one on board will take her tales seriously once I warn them of my lad's fanciful nature. And you two will stay well away from her.'

There seemed nothing else for it. If he was telling the truth, I was standing with Mr Dixon's blood on my skirt, wanted for murder. If Frank tried to clear my name, our captor would kill me instantly. Any way you looked at it, the prospect was bleak. Our enemy had trapped us into taking on the roles he wanted in this little drama of betrayal and humiliation, and I couldn't for the moment see an end to it. Yet it was also clear that we had no choice if we wanted to stay alive a little longer. I crawled to the bundle and picked out the smallest of the jackets.

'At least have the decency to turn your back,' I said, fighting back a sob. I wasn't going to let the sailor report back to our enemy that I was broken so easily.

The three of them looked away as I changed. I then stared at the bulkhead as Frank and Pedro followed my example.

'Come here,' the sailor said, beckoning me forward. 'Turn around.' He grasped my hair and yanked it back into a sailor's pigtail. 'Now you look the part.' Then, sweeping up our clothes, he called over his shoulder: 'Follow me, girl. You two, up on deck. Captain Barton wants to meet the new hands. And remember, not a word or you'll never see your little sweetheart here again. See, if there's no girl, there's no proof any of this happened, so don't even think of trying to outwit me.' Resting a big hand on my neck, he gave them an evil grin and watched them climb out of sight.

Alone for the first time, the sailor seemed less at ease. I guess his manner had been an act to convince Frank and Pedro he had everything under control, but he was obviously aware of the personal risk he was taking smuggling us aboard. In a hurry now, he led me up several steep ladders to the upper gun deck. The big open space that housed the cannon, as well as accommodating many of the men, was empty just now – everyone appeared to be outside.

'We don't have long,' he said, showing me into a canvas-sided cabin in what I was to learn to call the bow, or front part of the ship. 'You're to sling your hammock and attend to any woman's business in here.' He pulled at the scarf tied round his neck, embarrassed to talk of such matters. 'It's in your own interests to keep yourself to yourself – safer for your friends and for you. If anyone asks, you say you're my apprentice, Jimmy Brown, got that?'

I nodded, too afraid to do anything else.

'You'll join the starboard watch; your friends'll be in the larboard so you won't be seeing any of them. In between other duties, you come back here, understand?'

'Yes.'

He raised his hand threateningly. 'You say, "Aye, aye, Mr Maclean."'

I swallowed. 'Aye, aye, Mr Maclean.'

'One of your main duties will be to help me with the stores. That means you'll be spending a lot of time down in the hold out of sight. Got that?'

'Aye, sir.'

My new 'master' pushed me in the small of the back, firing off orders and information as we went. 'You'll join my mess. We eat with the carpenter, the bosun, the sawbones, the gunner and his wife.'

'The gunner has a wife?' That sounded hopeful; perhaps another woman would take pity on me?

'Don't get any ideas: you're to keep away from the doxies.' He pushed his way past the rolls of hammocks swinging from hooks on the bulkhead.

'And you'll find you're not the only female on board – far from it. But you're the only one who'll appear on the roll as a boy, which'll get you your ration. I'm not sharing mine.' A bell rang. 'We'd better hurry up and show our faces on deck.'

Having reached the hatch, I climbed the first rung of the ladder before he grabbed me round the neck and pulled me back. He was very on edge.

'I'll be watching you,' he growled, face thrust in mine, 'every moment, every day, got it? If you give your true identity away by a careless look or gesture, then you're dead.' He was choking me. I tugged at his fingers. 'Got it?'

'Yes,' I gasped. 'Aye, aye, sir.'

'Good.'

With that, he stumped up the ladder. I scrambled after him, feeling light-headed. I could barely see out of my left eye, my lip was split, I felt sick and shaky, but if he believed he had broken me in already, he had another thing coming. He didn't know Cat Royal. I was biding my time, trying to work out who our enemy was and what we could do about it. For lack of alternatives with a face or name known to me, my mind had already circled back to the obvious conclusion. It was surely no coincidence that it had been Billy Shepherd who sent us to the *Honest Tar*. As for being squeamish about bloodshed, pehaps Billy was just baulking at breaking his word to me that he was not plotting to harm Frank. Perhaps.

Emerging in to the daylight after hours down in the hold, I was at first blinded by the light. Maclean seized my shoulder and pulled me to his side. All the men were lined up on deck, looking up to a raised area at the stern, to where the officers were gathered, awaiting the captain. It was my first time on board a warship and, even under these circumstances, I was overwhelmed. The *Courageous* was a masterpiece of modern engineering, a deadly killing machine big enough to carry seventy-four huge guns housed on two decks below our feet. Three masts sprang through the planks and up into the sky. Each was laden with billowing white sails. There were so many ropes stretching above, far more complicated than even the flies at Drury Lane; I wondered how anyone knew which one to touch.

Tearing my eyes from the seaman on lookout, perched on the cross-trees at the top of the main mast, I sought out my friends. I couldn't find them at first, hedged in as I was by tall men all waiting in a nervous silence. Shifting slightly to peer round Maclean, I spotted Frank and Pedro on the far side of the deck. And Syd was with them.

Syd.

In the perils of the last few hours, I'd almost forgotten that my friend might be on board. Did Maclean know about him? I glanced up at my captor but he was frowning, watching the officers warily. Having an ally Maclean knew nothing about might prove invaluable. I looked back to my friends. They couldn't see me but from Syd's angry flush and flexing fists I guessed he knew I was on board. I only hoped Frank had had time to tell him the whole story. If Syd exploded and revealed my presence to Captain Barton, I dreaded to think what the outcome might be. I didn't want my neck stretched by a rope from one of the masts – I liked it the length it was.

The door to the captain's cabin was now

thrown open and a man dressed in a salt-stained uniform strode to the rail to look down on us. Enter Captain Barton, Barmy Barton – and I was soon to learn that the nickname was well deserved. He had a shock of grey hair tied back in a black ribbon, a weather-beaten face, and eyes that failed to point in the same direction. Perhaps both eyes were on the alert for those demons Maclean had mentioned. He sniffed and spat on the lower deck. Immediately, a boy of my age dashed forward and scrubbed the mess away.

'Seamen,' announced the captain in a rasping voice, 'you have the privilege of serving aboard the finest ship in His Majesty's navy. I run a disciplined ship. There will be no brawling. No slacking. No drunkenness. Any dereliction of duty will be punished severely.'

I saw some of the old hands shudder.

'Obedience will bring rewards. Now, those of you who joined us in Bristol,' the captain glanced to the huddle of landsmen standing with Syd, Frank and Pedro, 'need to put your old life behind you. Understand, whoever, whatever you were before does not matter here. On my ship, my word is law. I am your father, your mother, your god.'

Silence met this insane pronouncement. Frank was frowning; I could tell he was composing his letter of complaint to the Admiralty even as he stood there.

The captain nodded to his first lieutenant, a severe-looking man with a hooked nose. 'Mr Lely, enter their names in the muster book and assign them their duties.' As the lieutenant moved to execute the order, he revealed the officer I had met briefly at the ball standing behind him. Gone was the smiling, relaxed Lieutenant Belsize who had been chatting to Mr Dixon in the Octagonal Room; in his place was a scared-looking officer standing poker-straight, ready to jump at the least word. Would he remember and recognize me? It seemed unlikely with my black eye and boy's clothing.

My speculations were interrupted as Maclean marched me forward to enter my name among the ship's company. As purser, Maclean was a cut above the common seamen so took me to the front of the line, well away from my friends.

'Ah, Maclean,' said Lieutenant Lely with a wintry smile, 'and who's this young lad?'

'My new apprentice, sir,' replied Maclean quickly. 'Jimmy Brown.'

I watched as one of the midshipmen, a young gentleman no older than Frank, entered 'James Brown' on the list. I was given the rating 'Boy, Third Class.'

'Doing him a favour, I take it?' commented Lely.

'Aye, sir. Giving him his chance.'

'Good, good. You, boy, I hope you'll live up to Mr Maclean's expectations.'

I bit my tongue. 'Aye, sir.'

'Move along then.'

We waited among the other hands as the rest of the new men were entered. I wondered what name Frank gave; whatever it was caused no concern, for his details were rapidly recorded and he was pushed on by the next man. When the formalities had been completed, a bell rang on the upper deck.

'F-fall in, n-new men, for the captain's inspection,' roared Lieutenant Belsize, finding a voice that he had not dared use in the civilized confines of the Assembly Rooms.

'Behave!' Maclean gave me a shove in the back towards the other boys. This meant that for the first time I was near Pedro. I took my place next to him. Frank and Syd were standing among the men. All three of them were watching me. I tried to smile but somehow my face had forgotten how to do it.

The captain began prowling down the line. He stopped in front of Syd, standing so close he was practically breathing into his face. Suddenly, Barton launched a punch at Syd's stomach. The blow fell but Syd did not flinch. His eyes widened for a moment, but then he continued looking over the captain's shoulder as if nothing had happened. Captain Barton rubbed his knuckles and chuckled.

'Excellent. So we have a new champion among us. I look forward to challenging the other captains when we arrive in the West Indies.'

Barton continued down the line. Frank looked worried as he approached – as well he might – but he was passed over with only a nod. The captain now reached the new boys. He paused for a moment in front of Pedro.

'Where are you from, boy?'

'London, sir,' replied Pedro fearlessly.

'And before?'

'Africa, sir.'

'Slave?'

'Freeman, sir.'

'Hmm, we'll see. Mr Lely, check the boy's claim when we get to Kingston. I don't want to harbour any runaways.'

The captain took a pace and one of his eyes fell on me.

'Who's this?'

My heart was pounding. Had he noticed already?

'Your name, boy?'

'J-Jimmy Brown, sir,' I managed to stammer. 'Purser's apprentice.'

'They should've called you Tom Thumb.' The officers standing at the captain's shoulder laughed dutifully. 'How came you by that black eye, boy?'

'I had an encounter with the press gang, sir.'

Maclean shuffled forward at this point, squeezing his cap between nervous hands, worried his deception was about to unravel. It was on the tip of my tongue to take a chance and blurt out my true identity, but then the mad glint in Barton's eye pulled me up short. This was a man quite capable of a summary hanging just on a whim, I was sure of that.

'Hmm, finely spoken. Can you read and write?' asked the captain.

'Aye, sir.'

'Where did you learn?'

Maclean stepped in. 'From his last captain, sir. The boy said he'd been in the merchant service.'

'Already been at sea then, boy?'

I looked at Maclean in confusion. 'Er, aye, sir.'

'Did you abscond?' Barton's face was darkening; I could sense the mad fury was never far from the surface. He gripped me around the throat as if to wring the answer from me.

'No sir, he was paid off,' the purser said quickly. 'Drank his wages and about to go home to his old mum when I met with him. Offered him a chance to join the king's service – he leapt at it after my lads got hold of him.'

The moment passed; Barton was back in control of himself. He let me go.

'A bit of luck for you, eh?' growled the captain, patting my shoulder as if for all the world he hadn't just been throttling me.

'Aye, sir,' I gasped.

Bit of bad luck.

Barton turned away. 'New boys, let us see what you're made of: first up to the cross-trees gets double rations for a week. On my word . . . go!'

There were five of us: four boys, including Pedro, and me. The others sprang to the main-mast. Pedro grabbed my arm.

'Come on, Cat,' he urged.

Feeling as if this nightmare would never end, I followed him across the deck.

'I can't do this, Pedro,' I said in despair. I was in no condition to start scaling anything.

'Course you can,' Pedro whispered, putting my hand on the shrouds leading up the mast from the side. They formed a kind of ladder. 'You've got to.

It's just like playing backstage – no higher than the flies at home.'

'Get on with you, boys,' barked Lieutenant Belsize. 'Didn't you hear the captain?'

Pedro began to climb the ropes with ease. I followed as quick as I could, struggling up to the cross-trees to where three smug boys and one worried Pedro waited.

'Now slide down the halyard,' bellowed Captain Barton.

Not having the foggiest idea what that was, I hung back to watch the others leap on the ropes used to raise the sails leading back to the deck. It involved a stomach-churning journey in the air without the reassurance of the rope ladder. Screwing up my courage, I followed Pedro down the halyard he had chosen, landing last on deck.

I felt quite pleased with myself for having managed this first task without breaking my neck. My spirits were improved by seeing the captain congratulate Pedro for coming first. I was smiling as Barton swung round to me.

'You, boy, what are you grinning at?'

I switched off my smile immediately and stood to attention.

'You've nothing to grin about: that was the worst display of skylarking I've seen in a long while. I thought you'd said you'd been at sea before?'

'Sir?' I wished the deck would open and swallow me up.

'You climbed the rigging like an old woman. You've clearly not had enough practice. Ten more times up and down. Mr Lely, see that he does it!'

'Aye, sir.' I felt a prod in my back from the lieutenant. 'Off you go, lad. Look lively.'

My arms were shaking as I began the weary climb back up. I could feel my friends watching me, desperate to help, but they could do nothing. It just had to be endured. When I reached the top, my hands were raw. Too much sitting around at Boxton had softened them.

Boxton. Had I really once sat in a drawing room worrying about being bored? I let out a strangled laugh. The sailor on watch gave me a funny look.

'Here, son, take a nip of this,' he said, thrusting a bottle in my fist. 'Just don't let them see.' He jerked his head to the quarterdeck where the officers were now pacing, minds turned to other matters than one sluggish cabin boy.

I took a swig. A fiery liquid burned its way down my throat and into my empty stomach. It certainly pepped me up, but did not help my already clumsy fingers to grasp the ropes.

'Thanks! See you in a minute.' I gave him a tired smile and began my descent.

By my sixth ascent it was getting dark. Mr Lely chivvied me along half-heartedly and only when the captain was watching. When I reached my friend on the masthead, a bell rang.

'Ah, you again, is it?'

''Fraid so.'

'That's the bell for supper,' said the sailor. 'Almost end of my watch.'

The crowds on deck thinned as the men disappeared below to eat. My stomach growled but I did not need to be told that I wasn't going to be let off completing my punishment just to satisfy my hunger. I paused for breath, my head swimming. The bottle was thrust in my hand again.

'Thanks, but no thanks,' I panted. 'Can't hold my drink.'

The sailor laughed. 'That's all there is on board, lad. You'll have to get used to it quickly.' He held out a hand to steady me. 'Easy there. The deck don't make a soft landing.'

'Thank you, sir.' I closed my eyes, fighting a losing battle with exhaustion.

My words made him laugh all the more. 'No need to call your shipmates sir, Tom Thumb. You can call me Harkness.'

'Boy! Get down here or you'll get the lash!' bellowed Mr Lely, seeing me clinging to the mast like barnacle.

So tired that I was now reckless, I slid down the halyard as fast as Pedro had done. Only four more to go.

Harkness had gone when I reached the top again, leaving the masthead temporarily unmanned. I hugged the mast for a moment, watching the stars come out, swaying dizzily overhead. I hadn't had any time to give thought to where we were but, from what little I could see in the gloom, we were already far out to sea. How had we ended up in this mess?

Careless of the consequences, I sat down on the yardarm, twining myself around a rope. Thankfully, there was no one to see me sobbing with tiredness. Mr Dixon: dead in all likelihood. My favourite footman, Joseph, injured, I knew not how badly. Pedro, Frank and I caught in this horrible trap. I couldn't see how I'd survive this: I just wasn't strong enough. I was a girl trying to do a man's work.

'That's enough, Cat!' an unsympathetic voice struck up in my head. 'You've always said you're as good as a boy; now prove it!'

'But I can't!' I wailed into the night.

'Oh, yes, you can. You never had a soft life at Drury Lane so why expect one here? You've been told to climb a few ropes, not swim the Atlantic. Get on with it!'

Growling at my unforgiving self, I struggled to my feet. Just as I placed my hand on the rope, a tune struck up below. It was Pedro – it had to be – I recognized that violin anywhere. He was playing a sea-shanty we'd often sung together backstage. He was playing for me.

Right, I thought, it's time to prove what I am made of. If Syd still doesn't let me into his gang after this, I'll punch him.

SCENE 2 – TATTOO

Finally, thankfully, trip number ten came and I landed on the deck for the last time.

'Very good, lad,' said Lieutenant Lely, giving me a pat on the back. 'Go get your rations.'

But it was not to be.

'You, boy!' Captain Barton strode to the rail of the quarterdeck.

'Aye, sir?' I remembered to stand up straight.

'Learned your lesson?'

'Aye, sir.'

'Then you can take first watch on the mast-head.' He disappeared into the golden, candlelit glow of his cabin, accompanied by the smell of roasted meats.

I couldn't believe it. I gave Lieutenant Lely a desperate look but the second-in-command's face was set. It would take more than this casual cruelty from the captain to shock him.

'You heard, boy. Up you go again.'

How I managed to get up there, I don't know. All that kept me going was the thought that I wouldn't have to come down again for hours. Very little watching took place as I lay my head against the mast, shivering. I wasn't even sure what I was supposed to be looking for, or what I should do if I saw something. My main preoccupation was trying not to fall asleep. I also had an urgent problem of a most private nature that would have to be relieved sooner or later. Utter misery.

I distracted myself by cursing Billy Shepherd with all the foul names in my extensive vocabulary. If he was responsible for our plight, I was going to survive this and make him pay. I pondered suitable punishments, but nothing came close to what he had done. After all that had passed between us in Bath, I felt oddly betrayed. Why I'd come to expect fair dealing from a known villain was beyond me, but still I'd never thought he'd get someone else to do his dirty work for him.

At around midnight, the eight bells rang, signalling the end of the watch. I heard my replacement panting as he climbed up.

'Cat? Still with us?' It was Pedro.

'Just.'

He pressed a dry biscuit into my hand. 'There. It's for you.'

'You shouldn't have –'

'Forget it. I'm on double rations, remember.'

'You've told Syd what's going on?'

'Yes. He was all for going to the captain but we persuaded him out of it until we've worked out if Barton is mad or not.'

'Oh, he's mad all right.'

Pedro rubbed my aching shoulders. 'Syd's on your watch so will look after you. You'd better get below: you've only got four hours before the next duty.'

I groaned and put my hand with practised ease in the dark to the halyard, but then I remembered something.

'Er, Pedro, where does one . . . you know . . .?'

Fortunately he understood without the need for more hints. 'At the heads – that's the front of the ship. There are some seats under the figurehead. I'd choose your moment carefully.'

'You don't have to remind me. Goodnight.'

I slid to the deck, landing with barely a sound, and attended to what was necessary. Feeling somewhat more comfortable, I made my way back to my cabin, passing Frank on the stairs. He gave me an anguished look but said nothing.

Maclean was waiting for me below. He snorted as I stumbled in.

'Taking to the life, eh?' he mocked.

I said nothing as I tumbled into my hammock. I didn't even nibble the biscuit; I was too tired.

It felt as if I'd hardly closed my eyes when I was tipped out of my hammock and ordered to take my second watch on the masthead. At least this time I had the reward of seeing Pedro as I climbed up to relieve him. He was difficult to make out in the dark but his hand felt frozen as he helped me up. The ropes were slippery with frost. He blew on his fingers.

'Frank and I have been thinking,' he whispered. 'Our priority is to get you out of here, somewhere safe. Frank says he knows the second lieutenant by sight.'

'Yes, I met him too at the Assembly Rooms but he hasn't recognized me.'

'Just as well until we're sure of him. Frank's going to sound him out, see if he can be trusted.'

I didn't have a good feeling about this. 'But what if Maclean finds out what you're doing? The moment I signed up as a boy I as good as declared my guilt – no one will believe that I was forced to go into hiding.' I cursed Maclean, then sighed. 'We didn't have time to think this through properly. I shouldn't've gone along with it; I should've stated my innocence there and then. Instead I walked into the trap prepared for me, Frank too when he gave a false name. Now we can't do anything unless we can find someone to believe Frank is who he says he is.'

'But we've got to try something. You'll not survive this if we don't.'

'I'm fine,' I lied. 'I'm doing my best,' I added more truthfully.

'We know you are, and you're managing very well considering you've been knocked out, starved and tormented by a sadistic captain in the last twenty-four hours. And don't punish yourself: you are not to blame. Frank and I should've looked after you better – at least that's what Syd says.'

I grimaced. 'I imagine he didn't quite put it in those words.'

Pedro squeezed my hand. 'Well, no, he didn't. He's in a boiling rage. Look, this is a mess right now, but we'll sort it out. You just keep alive and keep your secret.' There was a shout from the deck. 'I'd better go. Just hang on in there, Cat.'

It felt doubly lonely when he'd gone. All I had were the stars and my thoughts. My hopes of rescue rested on the character of a red-haired lieutenant once met in a ballroom. Fate was a strange thing.

I had never before given much consideration as to what the defenders of our nation, the seamen of His Majesty's navy, ate for breakfast. The hours before dawn were spent pondering this all-important question. I had two wishes: that it would be hot and plentiful. When the bell for the end of my watch rang, I was down that halyard at a speed that even Captain Barton could not fault. It little mattered if I had left the skin of my palms on the rope: I was so cold, I could feel nothing. For the first time, I willingly sought out Maclean, hoping he would lead me to food.

'Here's my lad,' Maclean said, steering me with a heavy hand on my neck into his mess, a space between two cannons on the upper gun deck.

Five men and one woman were seated on benches around a suspended table, with a mess kid, or bowl in front of them. They looked up as we approached. The woman – the gunner's wife, I guessed – smiled at me and shook her head. She had kind eyes and looked no more than thirty. The gunner – a taciturn man – sat proudly at her side, letting her do all the talking for them both.

'The poor lamb looks blue with cold. Here, boy, sit by me and get this down you.' She thrust a bowl and spoon into my numb fingers and patted the bench beside her.

'Thank you, ma'am.' I sank down and began to bolt my food. It was skillygalee, a rich oatmeal gruel. Not up to Boxton standards but better than many a meal I'd scraped together in Drury Lane.

'Did you hear that?' she exclaimed to her husband. 'Called me "ma'am"!'

'Aye, I heard,' he grunted.

She smoothed the hair on the top of my head. 'Mr Maclean, I can see your boy and I are going to get on very well together. But you can call me Mrs Foster, dearie.'

'I'll say this for his last master,' said Maclean, giving me a warning look, 'he taught his boys to be polite.'

The conversation carried on around me about people and places I knew not. Bowl empty, I sagged back into my new friend's skirts and fell into a doze. Compared to the foul smells elsewhere on board, she smelt wholesome, even lightly perfumed, and, best of all, clean.

'Aw, look at the little thing. Worn out and the day's only just started,' crooned Mrs Foster, stroking my hair soothingly.

'Aye, the captain made him climb the mast ten times,' said Maclean. 'Good for his character.'

Mrs Foster tutted and said something unprintable about the captain. I completely agreed.

'Why not let him stay with me this morning, Mr Maclean?' she asked. 'I've some mending to do for the officers, he can keep me and the other girls company.'

Mr Maclean got up abruptly. 'Thank you, Mrs Foster, that's a mighty generous offer but my apprentice is eager to start his duties. We've the inventory to check today.' He gave me a kick in the shins. 'Come on, Jimmy.'

Reluctantly I scrambled to my feet. It had felt so good to have a motherly person caressing my hair that I didn't want it to stop.

'Goodbye, Mrs Foster,' I said, bowing to her and the company. This sent her into peals of laughter.

'Goodbye to you too, Jimmy,' she called after me, waving her hand.

Once out of sight, Mr Maclean backed me against a bulkhead.

'None of your fancy ways in here, or you'll feel the back of my hand. And keep away from the women. Got it?'

It seemed I could do nothing right – not that I wanted to please him, only spare myself further punishment.

'Aye, Mr Maclean.'

He gave me a box round the ear for good measure and pushed me down into the hold.

'Count the casks of peas. When you've done that, start on the water barrels.' He passed me a lantern.

'Aye, sir.'

'And I don't want to see your miserable face until noon, you understand? I'll be sitting here making sure no one disturbs you.'

I crept into the belly of the ship, relieved to be out of sight of Maclean, but fearful of what I would find. Reader, if you've not been in the hold of a ship before, you will not appreciate what a haunting place it is. You're not alone. For company, there are numerous rats, bold ones who are not afraid to sniff you over in case you offer them a tasty bite. The penned animals, destined to be slaughtered for fresh meat, moo, cluck and bleat mournfully, the smell of dung adding to the already noxious atmosphere. Then there's the slap and slosh of the water in the hold, reminding you of the watery grave awaiting just the other side of the planks. Few ships are completely watertight. Most have to keep a pump working from time to time to empty out the seepage before it damages the stores. And then there are the stores themselves: casks and barrels closely packed. It takes a small boy – or girl in my case – to rummage among them for the count and it's dangerous work too if something is not securely fastened.

But I was blowed if I could be bothered.

I had been abducted and threatened by this man. I was not going to lift a finger for him if I could get away with it. I looked at the list he had given me: a hundred and ten casks of peas. I crossed it out and put a hundred and nine – the cook had probably opened at least one since we sailed. I then squeezed myself into a space too small for Mr Maclean to reach, grabbed a thick stick to beat off any rats, and settled myself down to sleep. To survive this voyage I would need my wits about me and that is what I intended to achieve.

I slept surprisingly well and woke much refreshed, ready to do battle once more. Guessing noon was almost upon us, I crawled back out of the hold and handed Maclean the list. He looked at it and sniffed.

'Are you sure?'

'Aye, sir, I counted them twice over.'

He gave a humph but didn't dispute the figures any further. The only way to give me the lie was to do the work himself and you can guess what he thought of poking around in the dark.

After the noon meal I was allowed outside to participate in the cleaning, or what Maclean grandly called 'the swabbing' of the deck. All this nautical terminology was making my head ache. Incomprehensible orders were constantly being bellowed: belay this, reef that, up the mizzen, trim the top gallants. I felt as if I'd fallen among the canting crew. Thieves are well known for having their own language; sailors, it seems, have theirs too. Rest assured, Reader, this is not one of those stories which delight in befuddling you with such stuff. Laying my hand on my heart, I promise to keep such naval jargon to a minimum.

Scrubbing the decks had the advantage that Frank was able to make his way towards me. I could see that his knuckles were cracked and bleeding – not surprising when you consider that he never had to do a day's work in his life. It was murder on the knees – mine already felt rubbed raw.

'Where've you been all morning?' he muttered, trying not to move his lips.

'Sleeping,' I murmured. 'Between a cask of salted pork and next Sunday's dinner.'

He smiled in relief. 'Good for you.' He glanced over his shoulder to check Maclean wasn't watching. Fortunately for us he was arguing with the carpenter over by the steps to the quarterdeck. 'He's not offered you any . . . er . . . insulting behaviour, has he?'

Dear old Frank. Here I was with a black eye, grimy and doubtless smelling none too sweet, and Frank was worried for my virtue.

'No, Frank, he hasn't,' I replied, serious for his sake. 'I think that's the last thing on his mind. He's too busy trying to stop me being adopted by Mrs Foster and the other wives.'

'Syd wants a word.'

'I bet he does.'

'He's over by the water barrel.'

The seaman in charge of our cleaning party gave me permission to get myself a drink. I could sense Mr Maclean's eye on me as I wandered over to the barrel. I filled a mug and glugged the water. I can say one thing for it: despite being green-tinged, it tasted better than the stuff served in the Pump Room – that's if you ignored the little beasties wriggling about in the bottom.

Syd was coiling rope nearby. I walked past him and leant casually on the rail, my back to Maclean.

'Hello, Syd,' I said softly.

'What the 'ell do you think you were doing, Cat Royal?' he whispered furiously. If we'd been back in Bow Street in his butcher's shop, he would have been bellowing. 'Going down to the docks to save me! You should've kept well away. I can look after myself.'

'Yes, I know, Syd. You've done very well, being thrown on board this ship and whisked off to who knows where. We needn't've tried to help you. No doubt you wanted a change of scene, a breath of tropical air – do you the power of good.'

'It's not funny, Cat. What's 'appened to me is one thing, but you – this isn't right.'

'Course it's not, but what do you propose I do about it? I didn't ask for any of this, you know.' The ship dipped into a wave and I lurched against him. He discreetly set me on my feet. 'How did you end up here, Syd?'

'Mick Bailey.' Syd spat the words out as if they were poison in his mouth. 'And I earned 'im a fortune this summer! Didn't want to share it with me when it came to it; had me press-ganged instead.'

I resisted the temptation to tell him 'I told you so'. I'd warned him about his manager before now: nothing Mick Bailey did could surprise me.

'And what about you, Cat?' Syd murmured.

'The boys said you were set upon?'

'Yes, someone's paid Maclean to keep Frank out the way and I'm the hostage for his good behaviour.'

'I'm goin' to kill 'im.' Syd wrung the rope in his fists, glaring at Maclean.

I had feared this would be Syd's approach.

'No, you're not. If you want to protect me, don't start by getting us both hanged. I'm wanted for murder apparently; let's not make it the two of us.'

I knew this would be hard for Syd: realizing that he could only help me by doing nothing. I heard him sigh and he returned to neatly coiling the rope.

'So, 'ow are you managin'?' he muttered.

'I'm fine. Really I am. Yesterday was a bit of an eye-opener, but today's been pretty good so far.'

'If there's anything –'

'I know. You don't have to say. I know.'

'Oy, squirt!' I felt a sharp pain as something lashed across my shoulders. I spun round to see one of the bosun's mates, burly individuals whose job it is to whip slackers into a more industrious frame of mind, threatening me with a length of rope. 'Get back to work: this ain't no pleasure cruise.'

Syd sprang in front of me, which was far more effective than the whip in making me move. This was the wrong fight for him to pick.

'Aye, sir. Sorry, sir. Feeling seasick,' I said with a realistic retch. I knew only too well what that felt like, being a poor sailor.

The bosun's mate took a step back, worried I was about to puke over his spotless white trousers.

'Tom Thumb drank the water with nothing in it,' chipped in Harkness, my friend from the masthead, who had come to see what was happening.

'That'll kill you, young'un,' said the mate, shaking his head. He looked at me more closely. 'You're the one who had to climb the mast ten times last night, ain't yer?'

'That's right, Nightingale, up and down like a squirrel he was,' confirmed Harkness.

The mate took a step nearer. I flinched back,

Syd clenched his fists, but Nightingale only wanted to whisper some advice in my ear.

'Listen, Tom Thumb, keep out of the captain's way. Look busy even if you ain't. Don't drink that poison,' he nodded to the water, 'without a shot of rum to purify it. Understood?'

'Aye, sir.'

'Now, get back to work.'

'Aye, sir.'

As I holystoned the deck, scraping the timbers smooth, I reflected that Nightingale had just given me more sound advice in one short speech than most people give in a lifetime. There were more friends at hand than I had imagined.

Over the next few weeks, our ship sailed swiftly westwards, blessed with favourable winds. At first, any strong swell brought a recurrence of my seasickness but slowly I became accustomed to the unsettling motion of the vessel and found these bouts grew less frequent. It is strange how you can become used to the most horrible circumstances, even take some pleasure in them. I had never travelled so far in my life and could not help but feel excited by the prospect of visiting the warmer climes of the West Indies. I derived some comfort from the fact that I had successfully avoided Barmy Barton. The captain had not stopped unleashing his cruelty on the ship's company, but fortunately these thunderbolts fell elsewhere. One midshipman was lashed for being late for his watch. Six seamen were given three nights in the brig and no rations for drunkenness. The carpenter was scolded for hammering when the captain was asleep. Barton possessed a tormented soul, for every little thing drove him wild with rage out of all proportion to the offence. I couldn't help wondering what ghost from the past haunted him, giving him no rest. Maclean had hinted at something, but he was the last person I was going to ask for an explanation.

And yet, Barton could also be disconcertingly charming; with him, you could never tell which way the wind was blowing. Pedro had become something of a favourite. In addition to double rations, he was summoned every evening to play to the officers' mess. Music soothed our master like nothing else could. This gave Pedro the very welcome perk of eating his share of the captain's leftovers – far better stuff than the ordinary seamen's diet. He was now rarely expected to take part in the night watch, being groomed instead to be the ship's musician. He accompanied the sailors as they raised a sail or wound the capstan, varying the beat to suit the task. On these occasions, the ship felt a happy place to be: an island of music and industry afloat on the blue-grey seas of the Atlantic. The seamen began to whisper that he brought them good luck: we had a fresh wind filling out the sails for many days. It was cold, but otherwise kindly weather for winter.

As for Syd, he had no trouble earning his place among the men. The secret of his boxing success was his agility and strength – excellent qualifications for a sailor. He had no fear of heights and soon numbered among the elite topmen, responsible for the very highest of the sails. I could hardly bear to watch him out on the yardarm with only a footrope to stop him falling.

In our free time in the evenings after supper, he taught all comers the basics of boxing – another activity highly approved of by the captain. It soon became a common sight to see six or seven men, stripped to the waist even in this freezing weather, puffing away as they pummelled each other. Syd had always dreamed of having a boxing school, but I bet he hadn't imagined it would be afloat.

At first, Frank had more problems finding his feet. He fulfilled his duties without distinction, not enough to earn either praise or punishment. Then, one day, he was handed a pack of cards. That changed everything. Taught the tricks of the trade back in London by one of Syd's gang, Joe 'the card' Murray, Frank soon had a devoted following of admirers. When it was discovered he could also read and write, he was suddenly very popular. Seamen of all nations demanded his services to write letters home to their wives, mistresses and mothers, holding them ready for when we met with the next boat heading back to England. As the main currency on board was grog, Frank could've been drunk all the time if he wished, so many owed him their ration.

So everyone was doing well – everyone but me. True, I had plenty of sleep, thanks to the continuing inventory of the hold, a most imaginative task on my part, but I dreaded my time in reach of Maclean above deck. He seemed to regard me as a useful vent for his frustration and I'm sure that the secret knowledge that I was a girl added spice to his nastiness. Mrs Foster scolded him for his gifts of undeserved blows and kicks but that only made it worse: Maclean accused me of bleating to her. I felt wretched but dared not say anything to Frank or Syd. I confided instead in Pedro; he knew enough of men's cruelty to understand that I just needed someone to talk to, that no one could help.

'The problem is,' I told him on Christmas Eve up on the cross-trees, the usual place for our private chats, 'that Maclean's attitude is infectious. I'm getting cuffed and pushed about by almost everyone now. If even my so-called master doesn't care two hoots for me, no one else will. It's nothing deliberate by the others, just a habit.'

Pedro nodded. 'So I've noticed. They don't respect you. You've got to earn your place somehow.'

'Oh yes, and how exactly? What can I do? Pick a fight with someone?' I could see Syd down below correcting the stance of one of his pupils. 'But that'd only confirm to them that I'm nothing when I get beaten to a pulp.'

'No, I don't think that's a good idea,' he said with a smile. 'Look, maybe Frank will get his chance to talk to Lieutenant Belsize. Maybe this'll all be over sooner than we think.'

'Hmm, maybe.' Pedro wasn't often guilty of wishful thinking but we both knew this was a long shot.

We fell silent. I stared out across the ink-black ocean, awed by the vastness of the world. The moon ducked in and out of clouds as if playing hide-and-seek. The gentle rise and fall of the waves felt like a mother rocking the ship to sleep. Letting the mood creep into my soul, my problems diminished, seeming small matters compared to the beauty of the starlight sea. The peacefulness made me feel more hopeful than I had for some days.

'Maybe we should wait till we make port,' I suggested. 'Harkness said we're not far from Bermuda. I think we stand a much better chance on land as long as it's got a decent sized port and other ships calling in.'

'How will that help?'

'It'll give me the chance to get away and then Frank will be free to tell everyone the truth.' The plan seemed to take shape as I spoke. 'I could try to slip off, change back into a girl and catch a ship home from there.'

Pedro did not look convinced.

I ploughed on regardless. 'No, no, it's a good idea really. They can't recapture and punish a girl for the desertion of Jimmy Brown, can they? If Frank writes a letter, I could take it to the duke and let him know what's happened.'

Pedro shook his head sceptically. 'And how do you plan to pay for this? I don't fancy your chances adrift in a seaport on your own with no money. That's if someone doesn't recognize you and arrest you first. And you can't think we'd let you go alone. If one of us comes with you, likely as not we'd be caught and flogged for trying to jump ship.'

He was right: I was fooling myself; it was a reckless scheme. At least on the *Courageous* I had the protection of my friends and I would not want them to follow me and end up in worse trouble.

'Frank's going to send a letter home in any case, if he can smuggle it away without Maclean noticing,' Pedro added. 'Once that's gone, he's going to have a word with Lieutenant Belsize.'

'Hasn't it occurred to you that Belsize might be in on this?' I'd had plenty of time to think such gloomy thoughts down in the hold.

'What? Why?'

'Well, all I knew about him before coming aboard was that he was talking to Billy Shepherd at the ball. That's not good. If they know each other, he could be part of the conspiracy. He might even be one of the disappointed suitors wanting to get the catch of the season out of the way. Billy mentioned that most of the young men in Bath hated Frank. Maybe they schemed together to do this to us? And to get us all on board must've involved more than Maclean, surely?'

'I don't know; in the dark with some hired thugs, Maclean might've been able to pull it off. And are you so sure that Shepherd is behind it? What does he stand to gain?'

Pedro was voicing my own doubts. I tried to put the case I had made to accuse Billy. 'Revenge, for one thing.'

'But I thought that you and he were . . . well, you know . . . on better terms these days? I would've thought he'd be waiting to see how that all works out before taking the drastic step of banishing you to sea.'

Pedro's words recalled that kiss and the promise that there was more to follow. It did not seem likely that Billy was this angry with me. But I had a second point to offer in my case.

'Maybe, but this isn't about me, is it? Frank's the target. And Billy would know that concern for me would keep Frank in check. He'd be more interested in getting Avon money from Dixon than flirting with me.'

'But Maclean said his employer didn't want a knife in the ribs for Frank; wouldn't that have been more in Billy's style if he wanted Dixon to come into his inheritance?'

'I don't know. I don't think I know Billy as well as I once did.' I blew on my fingers. The night was cool even though we were travelling south. 'And if not him, then who?'

'Well, who else stands to gain from all this?'

'Mr Dixon, of course, but he might be dead – not very clever if he's behind it.'

'Who's next in line then?'

'No idea; you'll have to ask Frank. But I suppose it would make sense for that lucky man to wipe out the two people standing between him and a dukedom.'

After what seemed an eternity at sea, the New Year saw us approaching the port of Hamilton on Bermuda Island. I wondered what it would be like, my first view of a world beyond Europe. At Drury

Lane, backdrops depicting exotic islands had always been painted with fanciful palaces festooned with lush fruits and flowers. Remembering these images, I passed the time on duty imagining myself lying in a hammock on a white sand beach eating peaches and grapes. The truth, of course, turned out to be somewhat different.

Having caught a glimpse of a chart with the islands tiny specks in the expanse of ocean, I had to take my cap off to the navigators: they had managed to get us here with nothing more than sextant, clock, sun and stars to help them. Hamilton hardly looked worth their efforts – not a good place to launch an escape attempt, being only a collection of makeshift houses around a harbour. Palm trees fringed the surf like up-ended ragged broomsticks. All in all, I had been hoping for something more inspiring for my first experience of distant lands.

A pilot came on board to see us through the reefs. A holiday mood stole over the crew as everyone anticipated shore leave after weeks of being cooped up with each other. Even sour

Maclean brightened up considerably, donning a fresh shirt and trousers as Hamilton came into view. This caused Mrs Foster some merriment.

'He has a special friend,' she whispered to me, 'a lady met on his last stopover. I think he expects her to be waiting for him. I am afraid your master is a romantic at heart, Jimmy.'

I found it hard to imagine anyone wishing Maclean to call; I'd run in the opposite direction. But I kept this observation to myself.

'Yes, a romantic. You'd never know it now but he was once in training to be a priest.'

'What!' I couldn't imagine anyone less godly.

'Ah, it rankles still with him; he rarely speaks of it.' Mrs Foster looked almost sad for him. 'Forced from that path by poverty, he said. Took to the bottle and cards like so many do.'

'He would never have made a priest,' I said bitterly.

She patted my face tenderly. 'You are too young to understand, Jimmy, but many of us have to live on when our dreams are crushed. It can spoil the best of us.'

Lieutenant Lely signalled for the shore party to prepare to disembark.

'Are you going ashore, Jimmy?' she asked as the boats were lowered. Maclean had appeared to have momentarily forgotten me, such was his eagerness to see his girlfriend, but he now overheard Mrs Foster's comment and that brought him back to himself. He realized that he couldn't leave me alone in port.

'Can't trust him, Mrs Foster,' he said, cuffing me around the head to punish me for his forgetfulness. 'He'll drink himself stupid like he did in Bristol.'

'Then leave him here with me,' said Mrs Foster. 'I'm not going ashore today.'

That wouldn't do either. Maclean rounded on two sailors standing in line for the boat.

'Here, Harkness, Nightingale, will you take my boy with you? Keep a close eye on him for me and bring him back in one piece?'

Harkness, my friend from the cross-trees, and Nightingale, the burly bosun's mate, seemed surprised by this sudden outburst of fatherly concern, but they agreed readily enough when some coins appeared in their palms. Mrs Foster nodded in approval, muttering something about it being about time too.

'You're not to let him out of your sight, understand?' stressed Maclean. 'And I'll give you double that if he comes back safe and sound.'

Having despatched me into the care of my two guards, Maclean went in search of Pedro and Frank. A short conversation with the bosun resulted in my two friends being held over until the second shore leave. As ill luck would have it, Syd was already destined for tomorrow's party. That left me with no allies, just as Maclean intended.

As a final thought, Maclean took me aside.

'Listen, you little minx, don't try anything. I expect your friends'll think they can get word back to England, but it won't work. If they try to send a message, I'll get to hear of it and you'll be very, very sorry. Got that?'

Maclean looked me over, roughly buttoning my jacket to the neck. 'Go to the inn with those men, act your part and come back on time. Do nothing to draw attention to yourself.'

With that parting endearment, he handed me back to Harkness.

The sky was an unpromising iron-grey as we landed in the boat at the harbour. Where were the sunny tropical skies I'd always imagined? It appeared that January in Bermuda was not a good time to visit. Harkness and Nightingale, however, were not disappointed: they planned to go straight to the nearest inn and leave tourism to others. My pleas to be allowed to wander fell on deaf ears.

'Nay, lad, you're coming with us,' Harkness said. 'We'll teach you to drink like a real sailor.'

This was one skill I had no intention of mastering but my protests only encouraged them. They practically dragged me into a tavern, thumping a mug down on the table in front of me.

Now, Reader, I have always been of the opinion that strong drink makes men fools, rotting their gut and dulling their wits. To be honest, I would've preferred a cup of tea but could hardly request such luxuries here. I sipped the brew slowly, trying to consume as little as possible. Harkness fell into conversation with the comely barmaid, her skin as dark as the beer she served; Nightingale wandered over to a table in the corner where a crowd of men were gathered. Something seemed to be happening but from the occasional cries of pain and jeers I wasn't sure I wanted to see.

'Who's the boy?' the maid asked after a while, peering past Harkness to look at me more closely. When I turned away she interpreted it as shyness. 'Aw, Honey, no need to be 'fraid of Mary Belle: you be too young for mah taste. Come back in a few years and maybe then we see!' She gave a throaty laugh and blew me a kiss.

Harkness pretended to snatch the kiss from the air and clapped it on his lips. 'Now, now, Mary Belle, I don't want you corrupting my little friend here with your boldness. If you're giving away favours, here's a mouth that needs them.' He gave her a hearty kiss, inducing much more laughter and wriggles from the maid. I turned my eyes away in embarrassment, gulping my drink in order to avoid looking at them.

Five minutes later, Nightingale was back. He dug Harkness in the ribs, distracting him from his tête-à-tête with the maid.

'I think I'll spend Mean Maclean's money on one of those.' He nodded to the corner.

Mary Belle rose from Harkness's knee, stroked my face in passing and returned to her bar duties.

'What's that?' queried Harkness, eyes still on the friendly maid. Nightingale grabbed his shoulder and turned him to face the other way.

'Over there, mate.'

In the corner sat a foreign-looking man, Oriental I guessed, with a tray of equipment in front of him like a barber.

'He's doing tattoos. He'll give you anything you want.'

I burst out laughing. There had been a fashion for tattoos started by Captain Cook when he brought back stories of the wild men of the South Pacific. All the rich men had had one – even royalty, they said. It seemed the practice was now spreading to us lower orders.

'What's so funny, Jimmy?' Nightingale growled.

'Nothing.' I drowned my laugh quickly in a mouthful of ale. 'What are you going to ask for?'

He scratched his head for a moment. 'Well, I want something to impress the ladies. A bear, perhaps?'

I shook my head. 'Too clumsy.'

'A tiger?'

'Maybe. A bit too fierce perhaps?'

He heard the doubt in my voice.

'How about a wild boar?' suggested Harkness.

'Oh yeah,' I snorted. 'A pig, very appropriate. That'll really impress them.'

Nightingale clipped me playfully around the ear. 'Less of that cheek.' He turned back to Harkness. 'But he's right. I know – a stallion!'

Pleased with his choice, he was soon huddled in the corner with the artist, his forearm outstretched.

I yawned and drank a little more. It must be strong stuff: my head felt as if it were muffled in hot towels. Harkness refilled my mug.

'What are you going to go for?' I asked sleepily.

'I don't know, son. Maybe I'll have a heart with my wife's name: Jennie. Yeah, I think that'd be good.'

'You'd better make sure he spells it right.' I drew the name in the dirt on the tabletop for him. 'Your wife won't be impressed if you come back with some other girl's name on your arm.'

He squinted at the letters, memorizing them slowly. 'Thanks, lad. What about you?'

'Oh, I don't want one.' I now rested my head on my arms. Though if I had really been a boy, I thought blearily, it would have been amusing to have a tattoo. My friends in Covent Garden would be green with envy.

'What about a squirrel? You go up and down the rigging like one sure enough.'

'No, no.' Harkness seemed strangely blurred. I closed my eyes. 'If anything, I suppose I'd have a cat. But really, I don't want one.'

'What about your sweetheart's name? I bet you left a girl pining for you in London, eh? What's her name?'

My disguise required some proof of my masculinity it seemed. 'My girl? Her name's . . . her name's Pansy, but I don't want that either.'

With these last fatal words, I fell asleep.

I woke suddenly some time later to find someone gripping my shirt collar, pressing my head down on my arms. I struggled, thinking Maclean had got hold of me again, but then heard Nightingale laughing.

'Keep him down, boys. We're giving Tom Thumb a treat! We're going to let his Pansy know what a little pussycat he is.'

'Get off me!' I squealed. My collar was wrenched back, exposing my neck, and then a sharp pricking pain pierced my shoulderblade.

'Now, now, Jimmy, you mustn't squeak like a girl. Take it like a man,' said Harkness, roaring with laughter. 'We're giving you one on the house!'

My resistance was futile, only serving to attract the rest of the inn's customers to enjoy the show. Finally, I was allowed up. I quickly buttoned my shirt up to the neck.

'Don't you want to see what we've done?' asked

Nightingale, handing the smiling tattooist a handsome tip. He then showed off his rearing stallion to me. Its hooves seemed to paw the air as he flexed his muscles. The artist had been good.

'No I don't, you . . .' (I'm afraid the rest of the sentence has to be censored). My shoulder ached furiously and I was filled with dread that I now had something unspeakable that I'd have to carry with me for the rest of my days. Of course I wanted to see, just not here in front of all these strangers.

But Harkness and Nightingale thought it all a splendid joke. They slung their arms around my neck and swayed down the street with me between them, singing and shouting. They considered that they'd done me a favour and we'd all had a roaring good time of it.

Well, at least I was now well and truly one of the lads.

SCENE 3 – FIGHT

We arrived back on board in the early hours of the morning, just managing to catch the last boat before it departed for the ship. Pedro, Syd and Frank were waiting anxiously for me, wasting time they should've spent in their hammocks. Assuring them that I was fine, I ducked below to the privacy of my cabin.

Maclean was also on the watch for my return. Seeing me back safe and sound, he grunted with satisfaction and turned in. Once he was snoring, I cautiously lit a lantern and tried to twist to see what was causing the fiery pain on my shoulder. It was impossible. Without a mirror, I'd need the neck of an owl to look behind me. I'd have to find someone I could trust to tell me the worst. My prayer as I readied for bed was that I wasn't branded with the name of a flower for the rest of my days. I would die of embarrassment.

I sought Pedro out after breakfast.

'Can you spare a moment?' I whispered.

He was preparing for his shore leave, planning to earn some coins by playing in the taverns. We could all badly do with some money.

'Of course, Cat. What is it?'

'Come over here.' I dragged him to a quiet spot on the forecastle.

'This is all very mysterious. What's wrong?'

'Something happened last night . . .' I could feel my cheeks blushing furiously but I had to know.

'Not something bad, I hope?' he asked, leaning in a little closer.

I groaned. 'Pedro, I've been a first-rate idiot.' I swallowed my pride as I confessed. 'I . . . er . . . got a little worse for wear last night and my shipmates decided to initiate me in their boys' club. They did this.' I tugged at the neck of my shirt, wriggling my shoulder free. 'What is it?'

Pedro moved the cloth out of the way, then roared with laughter.

'Pedro!' I was frantic. 'It's not . . . not "Pansy", is it?'

'No. It's a kitten – a beautiful black kitten with green eyes.'

I put my head in my hands. 'How am I going to explain this? I can't imagine tattoos ever becoming fashionable for girls of my sort. I'm marked for life!'

'Nonsense!' said Pedro briskly. 'My sisters had lots of them; they were considered very becoming.'

'But your sisters lived in West Africa; I live in the west end of London!'

Pedro ran his finger over my new adornment. 'Really, Cat, it's very pretty.'

'Pedro, what are you doin'?' I heard heavy footsteps and Syd appeared beside us.

'Ssh!' we both hissed. Did he want everyone to hear?

But Syd wasn't listening; he was really fired up about something.

'And what's this I've been 'earin' about you last night, Cat?' Syd continued.

'Nothing. I've done nothing.'

''Ad too much to drink, they're sayin'.'

I shifted my collar higher, but too late.

'What's that on your neck?'

'Well, it's –'

Syd grabbed my arm and pulled the shirt down.

''Ell's teeth, Cat Royal, you've got a tattoo on your back!'

I tried to push him away, but his grip was too tight. 'Lucky it wasn't my chest, hey?'

'This ain't a jokin' matter. You've ruined yourself.'

I felt a surge of anger. 'Of course I haven't. It's just a tattoo, for heaven's sake!' If Pedro noticed my abrupt change of tune, he was too diplomatic to mention it. 'Anyway, it wasn't exactly my choice, Syd. I hate it when you talk to me like that!'

'Like what?' Syd was so incensed he appeared to have forgotten he was still gripping my collar.

'Like it's all my fault. Let go or I'll thump you.' I slapped at his hand.

Unfortunately, Harkness happened to be passing.

'Did you hear that!' he crowed. 'Tom Thumb's challenged the Butcher!'

Like iron filings to a magnetic, we found ourselves in the middle of a crowd of eager sailors. Bets were already exchanging hands.

'Thirty seconds: that's how long he'll last!'

'No way. Five, that's what I give him.'

'Five minutes?'

'No, you idiot, seconds.'

'Hey, hey!' said Syd, finally letting go of me and holding his hands up. 'I'm not fightin' the shrimp.'

'It's not up to you, shipmate,' said Harkness, clapping me on the back right on my tender shoulder. 'The little'un challenged *you*.'

I was about to declare my complete lack of desire to fight when Pedro stepped on my foot.

'Give him a few moments to prepare,' demanded Pedro. Syd and I rounded on him, speechless.

'Right,' said Nightingale. 'Clear a space there.'

I grabbed Pedro by the arm and pulled him away from eavesdroppers. 'Have you gone mad?'

'No, I've not. Weren't we saying only the other night that you need to earn the men's respect?

Think about it, Cat: if you refuse to fight now, you'll be bullied for the rest of the voyage. Take on the biggest man in the crew and they'll admire you for your pluck if nothing else.'

'But this is Syd we're talking about! Remember him: six foot of muscle, punch like a sledgehammer?'

'Ah yes.' Pedro gave me a most annoying smirk. 'But you forget you have one major advantage.'

'And what's that?'

'He won't want to lay a finger on you. In fact,' Pedro now frowned, 'I think that's going to be the main problem. If he doesn't make it look like a real fight, this won't work. There's nothing for it: you'll have to make him thump you at least once – goad him to do it.'

'You're telling me to ask Syd to punch me?'

'He's too kind to do any real damage –'

'You've clearly not been to enough of his fights if you think that.'

'You'll be fine. I'll tell Syd what he has to do.' Pedro turned towards Syd, who was standing looking puzzled. Harkness was doing a furious trade, taking bets from the excited crewmen.

I held Pedro back by his jacket. 'He won't do it, even if he knows why he should.'

'Exactly, so you've got to force him.'

'How?'

'Come on, Cat, you've one of the sharpest wits in London: surely you can think of something!'

He left to explain the plan to Syd. I rolled up my sleeves, deep in thought. I could see what Pedro was trying to do, but it wouldn't work. Only the utmost provocation would cause Syd to lose his control with me.

Oh no. I'd just realized what I could say.

'What's going on, Cat?' Frank appeared at my side, watching the preparations for the bout with interest. 'Who's Syd taking on?'

'Me.'

'What!'

'I know. It's Pedro's idea, not one of his best.'

'Pull out – stop this now!'

But it was too late for that. The men suddenly stood to attention as the captain strode among us. With any luck, I thought, he would put an end to this madness.

'What's all this?' Barton asked sharply.

'Someone's challenged the champion, sir,' said Harkness, shifting nervously like a boy caught with his pocket full of scrumped apples.

'Excellent!' The captain rubbed his hands together and looked around the circle. One of his eyes came to rest on Nightingale. 'Who's the challenger?'

'Jimmy Brown, sir,' Harkness replied hoarsely.

'Who?'

'The boy, Tom Thumb, sir.'

There was a moment when we all wondered how he would react, but the see-saw of his mood came down in good humour.

'Capital! I'll put a shilling on the boy being knocked out in the first round.'

The men cheered. I was pushed forward by Harkness as Nightingale stood as referee.

'Right, men,' grinned Nightingale, 'each round lasts three minutes. Nothing below the belt, remember!'

'Not fair!' called out Harkness. 'Tom Thumb can't reach any higher.'

A ripple of laughter passed through the crowd. The whole ship's company had gathered to watch. I spotted Lieutenant Belsize at the captain's shoulder. He went up in my estimation because he at least looked worried. Maclean stumped up behind to find out what all the fuss was about.

'Pardon me, s-sir,' stuttered Belsize, 'but is this wise?'

'Course it's not!' roared the captain. 'It's David and Goliath!'

Syd and I faced each other across the deck. With a rueful smile, I raised my fists. He shook his head.

'Come on, you big oaf, afraid of me, are you?' I jeered, trying to will him with my eyes to play along.

'That's right, Jimmy, you tell him!' shouted Harkness.

'Set to!' announced Nightingale, jumping out of the way.

I fell upon Syd, pummelling his stomach, doing absolutely no damage except to my knuckles.

'Fight me, you big . . . big girl!' I shouted. That

felt good. Even if my blows did nothing, I was enjoying the chance to let rip. I'd been bottling up my anger for too long.

Two big open palms started catching my punches and turning them away. Two big feet started to move around the deck. Good: I'd got some reaction.

'He's just playing with the boy!' complained some of the more bloodthirsty of the crew. 'Hey, Butcher, finish the whippersnapper!' He must've been one of those with a bet on me lasting no more than five seconds.

'Crewman, fight the lad properly or feel the lash!' barked the captain.

The mood of the crowd soured. The joke no longer felt so amusing with one of them threatened with punishment. I began to pray that Syd would take at least one swipe at me, though I knew that he'd think any number of strokes better than harming a hair on my head. I had to do something.

'Time!' Nightingale stepped in, signalling the end of the round. I fell back to my corner to where Frank was waiting. He wordlessly passed me a cloth to wipe my brow. He didn't have to say anything for me to know that he heartily disapproved of my antics.

'Thanks.' I splashed water over my face. 'How am I doing?'

'I'm not answering that. What's all this about, Cat?'

'Syd and I argued; someone got the wrong end of the stick.'

'What on earth were you arguing about?'

'My tattoo.'

'Your what?'

'I'll show you later.' I gave him a reckless grin.

'You're enjoying this, aren't you?' grumbled Frank.

'I would be, if Syd would just make it look like a real fight.'

'He won't; you know him.'

'Wait and see.'

Nightingale tapped me on the shoulder. I returned swiftly to the ring to the cheers of the crew. I began to understand why boxers might enjoy this; if it wasn't for the prospect of pain, to be the centre of all this adulation is fun. I bowed to my supporters.

'Come on, you big girl's petticoat, come and fight me man to man!' I shouted.

Syd shuffled back reluctantly. He leant towards me, hands hanging loosely by his side.

'Give it up, Cat. Let's shake 'ands and call it a day.'

'No. Barton'll flog you for refusing an order,' I hissed. 'Fight me, please!'

His blue eyes were full of anguish. 'I can't!'

'Set to!' bellowed Nightingale.

'Fight me, blast you!' I took at swipe at his jaw, lowered within reach. My knuckles connected with a crunch. The sailors whooped and cheered as I hopped away, shaking my hand in agony. Syd just stood there and rubbed his jaw. This was no good. Barton was now boiling with anger at the lacklustre performance of his champion. I'd have to use my weapon of last resort.

'You're weak, Syd,' I muttered as I attacked his stomach again. I hated what I was about to do. 'No girl . . .' (punch), 'could ever . . .' (punch, punch), 'fancy you!'

Still no response.

'You kiss like a maiden aunt . . .' (thump!)

Syd's fists curled; his body tensed.

'I like a real man . . .' (thump), 'like Billy Shepherd' (punch, punch). 'He kisses a girl . . .' (punch), 'properly.'

Whack! Before he knew what he was doing, Syd's fist connected with my face and sent me flying back on to the deck. I lay looking up at the rigging, seeing stars.

'The fight's over,' I heard Syd declare.

Two polished buckle shoes appeared by my head. 'Good show, lad,' said the captain. 'Have this.' He dropped a shilling beside me and strode off.

Frank rushed to my side and helped me sit up. 'What did you say?' he asked, horror-struck. 'Syd's run off. He looks furious.'

I groaned. 'Stupid stuff. I had to provoke him.'

'Well, you certainly did that,' said Pedro, taking my other side. 'I think he's blacked your other eye.'

'Go find him for me,' I begged. 'Tell him it

meant nothing, that I said the first thing I could think of to make him fight me.' I hadn't yet had time to calculate what harm I'd done to our friendship with my admission that I'd kissed his one-time rival: a lot more than a black eye, I guessed.

Frank nodded. 'All right. But no more of this, Cat.'

'Oh, I thought I'd take on all comers next. I just love rearranging my facial features.' I touched my puffy eye.

'Well done, Jimmy!' said Harkness, arriving at my side with a flagon of ale.

'Aye, I think you flew when he knocked you over. Spectacular, it was,' agreed Nightingale. A number of other men now gathered around us, slapping me on the back. It seemed Pedro had been right after all.

Frank had some difficulty tracking Syd down. Syd went ashore directly after our fight and only returned very drunk at midnight. Frank and Pedro ladled him into his hammock and came in search of me.

'Is he still furious about what I said?' I whispered as we crouched in a dark corner of the gun deck. Around us rumbled the snores of scores of men sleeping after too much carousing in the taverns of Hamilton.

Frank shook his head. 'You don't understand: he's furious with himself. He says he can't face you again.'

'That's silly. I made him do it!'

'No, Cat, *I* made you make him do it,' said Pedro glumly.

'But Pedro, your plan worked! I've never been treated so well on board. Everyone's proud of my black eye. Think how many cuffs and blows his one punch has saved me! And we both came away with our honour intact.'

'Not Syd. He hit a girl. He'll never forgive himself,' Frank muttered.

'Right, that's it: take me to him. I'm not putting up with his nonsense.' I stood up but Pedro pulled me back.

'Leave him. You won't get any sense out of him for the moment in any case,' he said. 'He'll wake tomorrow with one thumping headache.'

'Besides, don't you want to hear how I got on?' asked Frank.

I sighed and sat down. 'Of course.'

'Well, I found a tavern keeper who'll send the letter for me. He said there's bound to be a homeward-bound ship calling in soon.'

'That's good.' Even if we were still in danger, it was a relief to know that our reputations might be restored and the grieving Avons partially comforted. However, I still felt pessimistic about this plan. 'You were careful, weren't you? Maclean suspects that we'll try something.'

'Of course I was careful. No one saw. Trust me.'

'Hmm.' I wasn't sure. Maclean seemed confident he'd hear of any attempt to send word home. Hamilton was a small place and he'd been here before, but we had to try – whatever the consequences.

The following day, Syd was still avoiding me, nursing a hangover and a foul temper. Every time I took a step towards him, he shot off in the opposite direction. But he couldn't keep me away forever: we were on a vessel only 165 feet long and 45 feet wide – not much bigger than the stage at Drury Lane. Granted there were five hundred men to hide among, but he had no escape: we'd soon be at sea again. He didn't stand a chance.

That evening, during the recreation period after supper, I was taken along by Harkness and Nightingale to hear Pedro play. The seamen who weren't on shore leave were still feeling in a holiday mood. My friend was accompanying those who fancied themselves as singers or dancers. A Scotsman had just finished a fast, but not entirely accurate, jig and was taking his bow.

'Let's have a song!' cried Harkness. 'You, Nightingale – do you live up to your name?'

'Me?' laughed the bosun's mate. 'I sound like a crow. What about Jimmy the giant killer?'

'No, I can't carry a tune to save my life,' I lied, backing away.

'Nonsense, let's hear you,' cried Harkness.

Pedro raised an eyebrow, waiting for instructions.

'I . . . er . . .' It seemed easier just to get this over

with. 'How about '*The north-east wind did briskly blow*'?' Pedro nodded and struck up the ballad that had been popular at Drury Lane last season.

I had a reasonable voice according to Frank's mother, herself a trained singer; it was nothing to rival hers, of course, but sweet enough in its own way. I tried to roughen the edges and make it sound more boyish as I sang my tale. The sailors were good listeners, following each beat of the story, and I began to enjoy myself. The grisly tale ended with the hero being eaten by a shark – a fate with which these men of the salt sea could sympathize. I bowed to acknowledge the applause. They then began to debate the seamanship displayed by the hero.

'Stupid idiot,' commented one old sailor, 'he should've stayed in the boat. Sharks can smell you a mile off.'

'His lady must've been a buxom wench for him to forget that, him being a sailor and all that,' added another.

My choice of song seemed to please them. I was now besieged with requests but fortunately

Drury Lane had furnished me with many such tunes; indeed, I was surprised to find myself singing things I'd forgotten I knew. It was as if the door to a whole treasure-house was unlocked and I could pick a gem or two to flash before them. And in that bittersweet moment of the performance, it felt as if Pedro and I were back home, playing on stage. When our eyes met, I knew he was thinking the same. Seizing my chance of happy forgetfulness, I sang myself hoarse until my duties on the watch called me away. I left the impromptu concert feeling rather pleased with myself. Thanks to a punch from Syd and a few singing lessons, I no longer need be afraid of anyone on the *Courageous*.

Apart from Mr Maclean, of course.

And the captain.

Bad weather kept us in port, much to the relief of the men who valued the opportunity to drink their wages in Hamilton. I didn't relish the fretful movement of the ship on the stormy waters, even sheltered as we were. It brought back my old feelings of seasickness. I had spent my first ever sea voyage to France with my head in a bucket and I had no wish to revisit that particular scene from my past.[3] Fortunately, I was too busy to be ill. To keep me occupied but out of his way, Maclean sent me to work for the carpenter who was overseeing the ongoing task of repairs. The chippie was quick to assess my usefulness. A pot of paint was thrust into my hand, a strap lowered over the prow, and I was instructed to devote the next few days to touching up the battered paintwork on our figurehead. The bare-breasted wench with long flowing hair that graced the front of the *Courageous* was a great favourite of the crew so it was a task that carried with it some responsibility. She soon became my confidante as I chatted away to her. I decided that she must understand what it was like to be a girl among all these men. She was certainly very patient with all my complaints, particularly about Syd's behaviour since the fight.

That's men for you, she seemed to say, they

[3] Though if you are less squeamish than me and are interested to find out what became of one very sick ballerina, I refer you to *Den of Thieves*.

can't handle their emotions. Treat us women like children but when it comes to their own feelings, they are babies.

Those peaceful few days brought me a surprising contentment, considering everything. The smell of the paint summoned memories of scenery construction back home in the theatre. Even with the squally weather, it was far warmer than England in January. When the sun did shine, it brought out freckles all over my skin – not the fashion for ladies, I know, but I felt healthier than I had since retiring to the stultifying confines of the morning room at Boxton.

Ever eager for my welfare, Frank was quick to notice the change that had come over me. He swung down to join me one day. I was whistling merrily as I traced the raven curl on our lady's wooden brow. He said nothing for a moment, just watching me.

'What?' I said at length.

He smiled.

'What's up, Frank?'

'Nothing, Cat. It's just good to see you yourself again.'

'Hardly.' I gestured to my attire with paint-splattered hands.

Frank laughed. 'I didn't mean that. I meant that you seem back to the old you: you've found a place for yourself, a job that you like, made friends even.'

I rubbed my nose. 'I suppose I have. Sorry.'

'Why sorry?' Frank leant forward to wipe away the smear of paint I'd just left on my face.

'Well, I shouldn't be really. We're in a bit of a fix, aren't we?'

'You could say that. But my tutor told me that happiness in the face of adversity is the mark of a true philosopher.'

'Well, it's either that or I'm mad.'

'That's another possibility we have to consider.'

Frank took a spare paintbrush and began to dab at the figurehead. I bit my tongue: he was doing it all wrong. He would have to wait for his painting lesson for I had something I had been saving up to say to him. Now seemed the perfect opportunity.

'I've been thinking, Frank. As I said to Pedro

when we were still at sea, the only way out for everyone is for me to . . . well, to jump ship, I think the phrase is.'

Frank nearly dropped the brush. 'You can't, Cat! What will happen to you on your own?'

I shrugged. 'I don't know, but I expect I'll manage until you've unravelled this mess for me.'

A determined expression appeared in Frank's eyes. I could see he was preparing his arguments against; I had to move fast to convince him.

'You must realize that I'm the only one who can go as I can change back into a girl and disappear. Maclean can hardly set up a hue and cry for a female as that would reveal he knew about me all along and he'd be in serious trouble with Barton. But if you try and run with me, Maclean would make sure you were hunted down and punished for desertion.'

Frank said nothing for some time. I thought it safe to continue.

'I've been watching the boats here. I don't think it'd be safe for me to try and join another Royal Naval vessel. It'll have to be a merchant ship or one from another country. Then the best plan would be to get to Lizzie and Johnny in Philadelphia.'

Frank nodded. 'Yes, if you could get to them, they'd protect you until I've cleared your name and convinced everyone I'm still alive.'

So he was coming round to my plan then.

'Have you given any more thought to who might be behind this?' I asked, giving my lady's eyes a delicate curl of lash.

'I really can't say. Pedro told me you were asking who stands to benefit from getting me out of the way. If Will is . . . is gone, then the next in line is some second cousin, but he's as rich as Croesus and has his own title. He's never shown the least interest in me.'

'Hmm. I don't like the idea of you going back without first finding out who wants you out of the way so badly. They might try again and make sure next time.'

I could see that Frank was having a hard time imagining that anyone in his family wished him ill. Possessed of an incurably sunny disposition, he failed to see the shadows in others.

'But what if it's not about money but about revenge or jealousy?' he asked. 'That puts our friend Billy Shepherd well and truly in the running.'

'I know. But it's almost too easy to believe it's him. Have you some other enemies?'

'I don't think so. But, Cat –' Frank held my eye sternly '– forget this notion of jumping ship. It's dangerous to stay but it'd surely be lethal to go off on your own.' He waved his brush, splattering me with drops of paint. 'We all prefer to know where you are and what you're doing.'

'Idiot!' I flicked him back. A blob of black hit him square on the chin like a goatee beard. I burst into giggles. In retaliation, Frank gave me a beauty spot on my cheek. We were away. When we emerged for the noon meal, we both looked like Red Indians in their warpaint.

Afterwards, I strolled on the deck. There was a brisk breeze, the sun had come out and the sea sparkled an inviting blue as it lapped the pinkish sand of the bay. On the jetty some little children were fishing side by side, white, black and brown-skinned: they must've had parents from all nations as I guess is common in a transit port like this. It seemed a very peaceful scene; for a moment, I almost forgot that we were in danger.

Further towards the bow, someone else was gazing at the same view.

Syd.

He hadn't spotted me. I could see that he looked thoroughly miserable. It was high time that he forgave himself.

Sidling up to him, I caught his arm before he could escape again.

'Hello, shipmate,' I said casually.

He flinched and turned away.

'Syd, please!' I whispered, glancing over my shoulder. 'I can't bear this. I need you to talk to me.'

Syd stopped, his back still turned, shoulders hunched.

'You're my oldest friend; I can't cope with . . . with all this if you give up on me.'

Syd swung round, his face aghast. 'I'm not givin' up on you, Cat! I'd never do that! It's me: I'm the problem.'

'No, you're not. You are the kindest, bravest, most loyal friend a . . . person could want.'

He shook his head. 'No, I'm an idiot, not fit for . . . for any of you.' Suddenly, he thumped the rail with his fist. 'Cat, you warned me about my manager and did I listen? Nah, I thought I knew it all. If I'd 'ad more brains, if I'd been as clever as you, I wouldn't be 'ere; you wouldn't be in this fix. It's all my fault.'

'No, Syd, if anyone's to blame for what happened to you it's Mick Bailey. Your only mistake was to think the best of people.'

He gave a derisive laugh. 'Yeah, as I said, I was a fool. I dunno, Cat, I've always thought my first duty was to look after you, and what did I go and do? I punched you. I really 'urt you, not in play but in anger. I can't trust myself; you should keep away from me.'

'Listen, Syd: I made you hit me. You know that I can make you angry; in fact, I'm surprised you've not clouted me before now. You've been a saint to put up with me for all these years.'

Syd leant his elbows on the rail, staring out at

the children on the shore. We'd fished like that once upon a time on the Thames, me trailing after Syd with my line and bent pin, trying to keep up with him and the boys. We'd mudlarked together on the smelly margins of the great river of London, hoping for gold but finding only shiny pebbles and the odd copper. Here in the Bermudan sunshine, I stood as close to him as I could, our arms touching. No one saw him take my hand in his big fist.

'I'm sorry, Cat. There's no excuse for me. I'm not worthy of you.'

'You are worth a hundred of me, Syd Fletcher, so never let me hear you say that again!' I felt like crying because I'd made him feel so bad, but I refused to give way to tears: that would not help either of us. 'I didn't mean any of what I said.'

'And did you . . . I mean . . .'ave you and Shepherd . . .?'

I sighed. 'Yes. He kissed me once at a ball in Bath. I suppose I should've seen it coming, but I didn't.'

'Does 'e . . . 'as 'e asked you to marry 'im?' Syd asked delicately.

'Are you mad?' I felt a tear escape as I gave a hollow laugh. I rubbed it away. 'He's marrying a beer princess. I'm just an amusement for him.'

Syd seemed confused by the contradictory signals of a tear and laughter. 'But you're upset. Does that mean you'd like 'im to ask you?' I could see that Syd was exerting great self-control. All he really wanted to do to Billy Shepherd was thump him, not enquire into his marital prospects.

'Syd!' I protested. 'Billy and I would be as well matched as a fish with a pair of boots.'

'But 'e's rich, powerful now too. 'E's always liked you, you know, even when we were all runnin' around Covent Garden together as nippers.'

'Oh yes, I remember how he liked me. He used to pull my hair, steal my toys and trip me over. I imagine being married to him would be very much like that.'

Syd exhaled slowly and allowed himself a relieved smile. 'Good. I just had to check that . . .' He faltered.

'Check what?'

'That I still stood a chance. If I waited, that is. Look, Cat, I know you're too young and now I've got to earn back the right to even think it. And I know you don't know your own 'eart yet, and all, but I know mine. I'll wait until you're ready. Five years. Ten years if that's what it takes.'

Dear Syd. Here we were all at sea, me with a death sentence hanging over my head and him trapped in the navy and he was still planning our future together.

I didn't know quite how to respond. 'Thank you, Syd,' I murmured. 'You're right: I don't know my own heart yet.' I gave him a half-smile. 'But I do know that I wouldn't make anyone a very good wife right now.'

Syd shook his head, ignoring my ridiculous appearance and gazing only at my face. 'No, Cat, you'd be the best.'

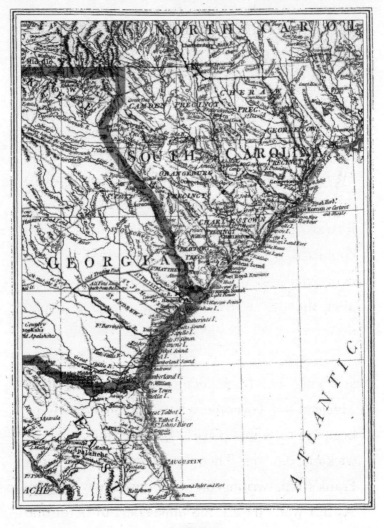

Act III — In which Cat learns who

is the real savage . . .

Act III

SCENE 1 – NIGHTMARE

We put to sea again the following day. After the holiday of Hamilton and its onshore attractions, I wasn't looking forward to being forced back into closer contact with Maclean. And I was right to be concerned. I'd only put a foot inside the cabin after the first watch when the purser swooped upon me.

'I warned you!' he whispered hoarsely, knocking me back against the gun carriage. Maclean stood over me, a letter in hand. Slowly, he began to rip it into pieces. 'You thought you could trick me, did you? Then think again.' A little bit of Frank's handwriting fluttered down into my lap. 'As if I wouldn't ask the innkeepers to be on the watch for this foolishness! Paid twice he was: once for taking the letter, once for giving it to me. His lucky day, he said.'

I swallowed a cry, watching our best hope being trodden underfoot.

'Do you remember what I told you?' he asked, hauling me up by my shirt front.

'Aye, sir.' I tried to keep my voice steady, but I was shaking.

'I said you'd be very, very sorry. And do you know what that means?'

I shook my head.

'Well, you're about to find out the hard way, you little witch.'

Pushing me in front of him, he hustled me down to the hold. We passed Harkness just turning into his hammock.

'Anything the matter, Mr Maclean?' he asked, sensing that I was in trouble.

'No, Harkness. I'm just teaching my boy a lesson. I'd appreciate it if you didn't interfere.'

Harkness gave me a pitying look. 'Aye, sir.'

Maclean shoved me down the stairs and opened the locked storeroom where I had spent my first few hours aboard the *Courageous*. He slammed the door behind us. He looked beside himself with rage.

'You think you're so clever, don't you, making yourself popular with the crew, getting your friends to write home for you? I think you've forgotten that I told you to do nothing to draw attention to yourself.' Maclean backed me into a corner, his breath heavy with the scent of drink. 'You can stay here until everyone forgets you exist. No shouting, no hammering on the door. If you behave, I'll bring you some victuals; if you don't, then perhaps you'll grow thin enough to slip out under the door. But before that happens, you'll be very good friends with this.' He took a bag from under his jacket and pulled out a leather strap with nine thongs. 'Do you know what this is?'

I shook my head mutely.

'It's a cat-o'nine-tails – a cruel thing. Stings like the fires of hell when it hits you.' He swung it in the air and flicked it against my legs. Pain sang out in nine sharp notes but I refused to make a sound. 'Like to feel that in earnest, eh?'

I shook my head.

'I thought not. Well, you stay here nice and

quiet and pray that I don't have cause to let the cat out of the bag again.'

With a parting cuff, he quit the room, taking the light with him. I curled up in a corner, wondering bitterly what I had done to deserve this. Whoever the enemy was who had unleashed Maclean on me, he was without a shred of mercy.

Time plays strange tricks when you are locked up in the dark on your own. It's very hard to guess how long you've been there. The only signs are your own hunger and the sounds of other people going about their business on the deck above. I knew from my inventory that my prison housed nothing more interesting than the cash boxes used for paying for supplies. They say that money opens doors, but not in my case.

My chief lifeline was Maclean's infrequent visits. He seemed to delight in tormenting me with news from above.

'I told the captain you were pilfering from the stores. He wanted to flog you but I persuaded him that this was a better punishment,' he said cheerfully on his first visit. 'Besides, he has some others to flog now.'

I said nothing.

'Don't you want to know who?'

I shrugged, trying to pretend I was indifferent.

'Those friends of yours, that lord and the giant you fought.' Maclean began to laugh wheezily, wiping his eyes on his cuff. 'Can't wait to see that rich boy's lily-white back taste the cat.'

I dug my nails into my palm. I wasn't going to say anything. I wasn't. My silence was the only power left to me.

'Shall I tell you how they earned the lash? The young lad tried to tell Lieutenant Belsize who he was, standing in his stinking rags claiming to be a peer of the realm. It was priceless. There he was, protesting about my treatment of you. But Belsize gave him short shrift, accusing him of a sick joke seeing as how the Earl of Arden had been done in on the eve of our departure. The lieutenant then grew suspicious and suggested your friend had been involved in the crime. Imagine it: accused of murdering yourself.' Maclean chuckled. 'Then the big man weighed in and Belsize had to call the bosun's mates to restrain the pair of them. Lucky for them it was Belsize they shouted at; he only ordered six lashes and half rations. If it'd been the captain it would've been six times that number and no rations at all.'

Maclean was annoyed that I kept quiet. I could see he was trying to think up how to scare me further. Well, if he wanted a whimper or a sob, he could fling his hat after me.

'Anyway, you'll find out how kind the captain can be yourself when I take you to see him. "Bring the boy low, Maclean," he says to me, "then bring him to me." Good man, our captain, a good man.'

I stared at Maclean's horrible face, concentrating my hatred on every inch of his flushed nose, purple scar and pimpled skin. He must have found something objectionable in my gaze.

'Keep those witch eyes to yourself,' he hissed, picking up the bowl of food he had brought with him. 'On second thoughts, you won't be needing this.' He tapped the weevils out and took a bite of the biscuit. 'And when you hear the drum, you'll know that your defenders are enjoying the kiss of my friend here.' He jiggled the bag hanging at his waist.

That numbered among the more pleasant of his prison visits. On his next he reported that Frank and Syd had taken their punishment like men, making not a sound. He complained, as he chewed more biscuit before me, that Nightingale, who had dealt out the flogging, had not been vigorous enough.

'Mrs Foster's been asking after you,' he continued. 'Said she couldn't believe that you'd stoop to thieving, but I told her she'd be surprised what vicious little boys can do. She asked me to tell you to pray to God that he changes your hard heart.'

'Oh, it's going to get a bit noisy down here,' he said on his departure, this time leaving me half a biscuit and a mug of watered-down grog. 'Gun practice.'

I fell on the plate as soon as he closed the door. Having eaten nothing for more than a day, even the dry biscuit looked appetizing. And he was right about the noise. First came the rumpus of the decks above being cleared for action. Partitions were struck down, possessions stowed, guns moved into position. The next few hours passed with the rumble of gun carriages, the thud of feet and the deafening percussive boom of shots being fired. My head rang long after the firing had stopped.

After more days of this, I began to look forward to the gun practice. It staved off the terrible feeling of unreality that took hold of me when left in silence. The darkness seemed to invade my mind, blurring the boundaries between me and it. I had the weird sensation that I was dissolving, like a sugar lump in tea. I feared I was going mad.

My dreams were insane enough, full of remembered horror. Scenes from the stage flashed before my eyes at breakneck speed: Caesar with the knife in his back, Macbeth's sword dripping blood, Hamlet pierced by a rapier, Mr Dixon holding up red hands . . . It was at this point I usually woke in a cold sweat, wanting to scream but being too afraid to open my mouth in case the darkness choked me.

'It's just a dream,' I chanted, hugging my arms to my sides. I was shivering, hot and cold by turns. 'A nightmare.'

I was kept in the hold a week in my feverish state, long after I'd convinced myself that I'd never see the light of day again. Finally, half-starved and as weak as a newborn lamb, I was dragged up on deck and dumped at the captain's feet. Someone threw a bucket of seawater over me. Barton prodded me with his foot as I lay on the deck, dazzled by the light and half-drowned.

'This, men,' he called out, 'is what we do to boys who steal. Lucky for him he's not a man yet, or he would've swung from the yardarm. Our stores are our lifeline. To pilfer from them is to take from your crewmates and put us all at risk.' He turned back to me. 'Have you learnt your lesson, boy?'

I dragged myself on to my knees, seeing nothing but his shiny toecaps. I wanted to deny the charge, but what could I do? It was my word against Maclean's and besides, there were all those made-up figures on the inventory – some of them were bound to be wrong. He'd catch me out one way or another. I nodded.

'Then you'll be on half rations and double duties for the rest of the voyage as a reminder. Now, return to your work. Take first watch on the cross-trees or it'll be back to the hold for you.'

There was silence on deck. Everyone knew it was an impossible order for a boy who could not stand. Was he hoping I'd fall from the rigging so he could claim it was God's punishment on a sinner? But I couldn't go back to my prison. I just couldn't.

Gritting my teeth, I looked about me for the mainmast. If I could just reach the shrouds, perhaps I could haul myself up somehow. Deciding I'd have to crawl, I slowly made my way through the forest of legs and collapsed again at the bottom of the rope ladder.

I opened my eyes briefly and saw Harkness holding Frank back.

'Don't get between the captain and a crewman,' Harkness muttered. 'It's more than your life's worth to cross him.'

Pedro was staring at me as if he could help me climb by willpower alone. But I couldn't move. I closed my eyes again. It was still a nightmare: I'd wake up in the morning room at Boxton and it would all have been a bad dream.

Then I felt a pair of strong hands lift me from the deck.

'Come on, Cat, I'll give you a ride.'

It was Syd. A murmur ran through the crew at his audacity.

'That's right: put your arms around my neck. Remember how I used to give you a pickaback 'ome when you were tired? Well, just cling on like that.'

I felt Syd heave himself off the deck and begin to climb the shrouds. Two bosun's mates stepped forward to stop him.

'Leave him!' barked the captain. 'Let's see if he can get up there without dropping the boy. Goliath coming to David's aid – most amusing.'

'You'd better hold on tight,' Syd whispered.

I leant my face against his neck. I could feel the fresh scars from his flogging through the coarse material: I must be adding to his agony with my weight on his back.

'Syd, don't – you'll get in more trouble,' I begged.

''Alf way,' declared Syd, taking a breather at the lower yardarm. 'Don't worry about me: just you cling on like a monkey.' I began to cry on his shoulder, hot tears running down his back. 'That's what you were like when you were a little'un,' Syd continued, 'a ginger monkey – always in trouble, into everythink you shouldn't, tryin' to be one of the boys.' We set off again, the deck swaying dizzily below as the mast swung to and fro on the swell. 'You never complained when you grazed a knee. Never cried when we teased you. Askin' to be let into the gang and me tellin' you "no", but you would keep on tryin'.' A sail flapped noisily as the wind buffeted us. 'You didn't realize but you always were one of the Butcher's Boys. There you were, askin' to join the gang, when all along you were the 'eart and soul of it.'

We had reached the cross-trees. Syd gently lowered me so I could slide off his back to sit with my arms and legs embracing the mast.

'Can you 'old on now yourself?' he asked.

I nodded.

'Just four hours, Cat, that's all you've got to do, then I'll be back to 'elp you down at the end of the watch.'

My grip felt so weak; I slumped sideways, feeling detached from my disobedient body. Seeing I was barely conscious, Syd stripped off his shirt and lashed me to the mast.

'There, you can't fall now, Kitten,' he said tenderly, stroking my hair.

With that, he descended rapidly to the deck. I listened fearfully for angry voices, the sound of Syd being punished, but instead I heard laughter.

'So, Goliath, decided to befriend David, have you?' asked the captain.

'Aye, sir,' answered Syd. 'I think my blow to the 'ead sent 'im silly. You saw 'im: 'e couldn't walk straight.'

'Hmm, how very sporting of you. Back to work everyone – at the double.'

Relieved, I lay my head against the mast. I

doubted that anyone else would've got away with doing what Syd had done for me. Fortunately, he'd amused the captain and avoided a second flogging. But I'd never forget what he'd risked. The Butcher's boys had chosen well when they made him their captain.

It took me over a week to recover from my incarceration. Indeed, it seemed to have knocked the stuffing out of all of us and for a while there was no more talk of escape. Frank blamed himself for sending the letter. I tried to tell him that it wasn't his fault, that the only one to blame for what had happened was Maclean, but he was having none of it.

'I won't stand for this, Cat. I can't bear to allow that man to use you as his whipping boy to keep me in check!' Frank told me as we sheltered from the squall in a quiet corner of the upper gun deck.

I was feeling wretched. Worn out with extra duties, I kept going with rations smuggled to me by my friends. I chewed now on a spare bit of biscuit, wincing as my sore gums twinged.

'You can't help it, Frank.'

'I know, I know. But how can I prove who I am?' His eyes glittered in the gloom. 'I feel so powerless! But if they believed me, this would all be over.'

I leaned back and closed my eyes. It was an intriguing problem: how to prove you are who you say you are when you are believed to be dead? Six weeks into the voyage and a couple of hundred miles from the West Indies and Frank no longer resembled the soft-handed lord who had visited the docks at Bristol: his fists were as rough as a labourer's and his clothes ragged and dirty. His curly hair was matted and his skin tanned a golden brown. He now had the air of a desperado or bandit from one of Mrs Radcliffe's tales. If Frank stood up on deck and claimed to be a highwayman, I'd believe him; but the Earl of Arden, a lad scarcely out school? You had to be joking. The navy had proved to be a most unorthodox finishing school for the young noble, but there was no denying he'd changed over the last few weeks, almost beyond recognition.

'You need to prove it, Frank, and for that you need time without worrying about me. You have to tell Belsize enough about your life, the people you know, your education, to prove it's more than a wild claim.'

Frank smiled grimly. 'You mean parse a few Latin verbs and quote Aristotle?'

'If you like.'

He put his arm around my shoulders so I could rest against him. 'That was always more your sort of thing than mine, Cat. But, if our lives depend on it, I dare say I could dredge up a few phrases.'

I yawned, struggling to keep my exhaustion at bay. 'Well, there must be something a lord knows that the common schoolboy doesn't.'

'Like what?'

He had a point. When you came to think of it, there was nothing special about rank, no magic powers attached to blue blood. In the stories I've read, the lord-in-hiding is always revealed by some indisputable sign: a strawberry birthmark or evidence of his innate refinement. Once this is revealed, there is no more dispute: estates fall into his lap like ripe plums, the princess marries him with no more to do. Unfortunately, though Frank has many virtues, he has learnt to blend in well with the common herd. I admit that's my fault. He has learnt more vocabulary from me than his Latin master – and I don't mean of the classical variety.

'I don't suppose you have a ducal mole or a strawberry birthmark?' I asked hopefully.

Frank chuckled. 'Saying "if found, please return to Boxton"?'

'It was just an idea.'

'Sorry, no. You're the one branded with your name, remember?'

I groaned. 'Did you have to remind me?'

'You mustn't worry about it. Father has a tattoo on his ankle too, you know.'

'Your father!' I could hardly credit it: the serious, sombre Duke of Avon concealing a risqué secret!

'Yes, he was quite the rake in his younger days before he met Mama. Had one done when Captain Cook first came back from the South Pacific. It was all the rage apparently.'

'And what is it?'

Frank was laughing now. 'A devil – symbol of a club he belonged to at the time, before he became respectable. He keeps it hidden – a trifle embarrassing, you must admit.'

I sat forward with a jolt. 'That's it!'

'What?'

'It's not your mark you need, it's his! Who else but a close member of his family would know such stuff about an eminently respectable peer of the realm? It'll give Belsize and Barton pause for thought if nothing else. They'll at least have to check your story; think of the consequences if they failed to take this simple step and their mistake was later discovered!'

Frank looked doubtful. 'You think Barmy Barton will listen?'

'It may take some time. You should go through the first lieutenant: Lely seems a reasonable man and we still don't know if we can trust Belsize. It would be even better if you raise the matter near a friendly port; it'll give Maclean less time to move against you.'

'But not against you. Maclean will murder you if he finds out what I'm doing. Just as he said he would.'

'Not if I'm no longer here.'

'I thought we'd been through this already –'

'That was before he shut me in the hold. I'm no safer on board than on the run. Next time he'll probably succeed in killing me. He'll tell Barton I've been stealing again and my heels will be swinging in the wind. Then he'll do away with you and Pedro to stop you blabbing. No, we all end up dead if I remain here much longer. I'm the biggest threat to Maclean, which means I'm the biggest threat to your safety too.'

SCENE 2 – STORM

Thoughts of leaving the ship had to be abandoned for the moment as our luck with the weather changed as we approached the Bahamas. The squall developed into a storm. The winds were so strong we had no choice but to run before them, heading north, far off course towards Florida. I fretted with every day that passed pushing us further from a friendly port. Life on board took a turn for the worse. We lost a man during the first night watch, blown from the yardarm like washing off a line. I feared for Syd, climbing up there with the topmen as the ship leaned before the wind like a drunkard staggering home from a Drury Lane gin palace. The deck was now a slope. Ropes were stretched from stem to stern to give us something to grab as we battled against the blasts of surf breaking across the planks. Dry clothes became a distant memory.

Most of the crew were depressed by the

weather, exhausted and battered as the days passed. There were two notable exceptions: the captain appeared positively to relish the battle with the elements. He could often be seen striding the quarterdeck, water streaming from his cloak, yelling defiance at the skies.

'Come and get me then!' he crowed, shaking his fist at the lightning. 'If you want to punish me, God, then strike me down!'

The lieutenants pretended not to notice their captain's behaviour but the God-fearing among the crew muttered mutinously that he was calling our deaths down upon us with his antics.

The other person who seemed to welcome the storm was Maclean. In our hours together, he spent much of the time resting in his hammock with a satisfied smile on his face. I would have sworn that he'd been waiting for the bad weather. It did not take a genius to work out that he had a plan up his sleeve.

The crisis came the third night into the storm. Barton had recklessly piled on too much sail and, under the pressure of the gale, the foremast snapped like a twig. All hands were summoned on deck to clear the debris. In the hurly-burly below, Maclean moved among the crew with a purpose that had nothing to do with the task. Suspicious that something was amiss, I followed as the men turned out of their bunks and struggled up the ladder, my eye on Maclean who waited at its foot. There was no call for him to go on deck – as purser he was spared such duties – but he was clearly planning something. Frank staggered by, still dazed with his snatched sleep. Maclean moved in behind him, tailing him up the rungs. Quick as an eel, I squirmed in line in front of Nightingale.

'Oy, Jimmy lad, this is no place for you,' bellowed the bosun's mate, grabbing my shirt.

I ignored him and emerged on to the deck in time to be deluged by an incoming wave. I clung on to the rope, searching frantically for Frank. When I spotted him, he was halfway across the sloping deck, Maclean just behind him, like two climbers roped together on a mountainside. The purser turned to look out to sea: a huge roller was coming in broadside. As it struck, Maclean kicked

Frank's feet from under him. From that moment, things began to happen in slow time. Frank crashed to the deck, lost his grip on the rope and began to slide in the wave towards the port rail, nothing but a piece of wood between him and the hungry ocean. Not even thinking of the consequences, I launched myself across the deck in pursuit, half sliding, half running, catching up with him as he collided with the side. He toppled backwards, about to go head over heels overboard. I grabbed his ankle in two hands and wedged myself against the side, holding on for dear life. His wet skin slid in my palms – his weight was too much for me to bear – I was being pulled over with him.

Suddenly, a large shape appeared at my shoulder, grabbed Frank's belt and hauled him back.

'You two, get below!' the man bellowed.

It was too late for that: a second wave crashed upon us. Crouching over Frank, I clung on to a belaying pin, letting the force of the water push me against the side. It was like falling under the hoofs of a stampede of horses. When the deluge passed,

I looked around me with stinging eyes. The man had gone.

'Man overboard!' I screamed, my voice pitifully thin against the wind. 'Man overboard!'

Two sailors heard my cry. They threw Frank and me a rope and hauled us back up the slope. We fell against the hatch.

'He's gone!' I choked as Harkness pushed me down the ladder.

'Who's gone?' he asked.

'I don't know – a big man – the one who saved us,' I gasped.

I felt sick with terror. It had to be Syd, didn't it? Who else but Syd would've risked his life like that?

Harkness pushed his way through the men who'd gathered around us and disappeared back on deck. The interval of his absence seemed to stretch for eternity. Frank was white with shock, having just stared into the jaws of death. He didn't seem to have realized what had happened. Harkness returned with Lieutenant Lely.

'What happened, boy?' barked the officer.

'We've lost a man over the side, sir,' I said, my

voice raw with horror. 'He helped me pull Frank back on board and then got washed away.'

To my surprise, Lely cuffed me round the ear, his face livid. 'What were you doing on deck in the first place, boy, putting your shipmates' lives at risk?'

I didn't care that he was angry with me. I only cared that my oldest friend was probably dead. I began to sob helplessly.

'Stop that snivelling,' Lely ordered. 'You're in the king's navy, not the nursery. Go to your hammock and stay there. The deck's no place for a boy in a storm. Harkness, find out who we've lost and report to me.'

I hid in my bunk, shivering with misery. The moment of the accident flashed through my mind, again and again. I couldn't believe it: I'd saved one friend at the expense of another. It was too much to bear; the whole thing was too much.

'Are you all right, Kitten?'

Someone stroked my shoulder. I was dreaming now, or maybe Syd had come back to haunt me? I sat up so abruptly I fell out of my hammock on top of a very wet but warm body.

'Syd! You're alive!'

'Of course I am, you daft Kitten.'

I hugged him so tight, I didn't care who saw us. Then a terrible thought struck me. Someone had gone over – if not Syd, then . . .?

'Who was it?' I asked.

Syd shook his head sadly. 'Nightingale.'

'Oh no. It's all my fault!' I clung on to Syd, finding comfort in his strength. I wished I could just close my eyes and let him sort everything out for me.

'No, it's not.' Syd shook me by the shoulders. 'Listen, you're a 'ero, Cat: you saved Frank. Nightingale was a fine man; 'e did what any self-respectin' sailor would do: 'e went to the aid of 'is shipmates. 'E took the gamble and lost it; that isn't your fault. Curse the weather, curse fate, but don't blame yourself.'

'Blame Maclean,' I muttered, pulling myself together. I quickly told him what I'd seen. 'Syd, you've got to protect Frank. After this failed attempt, Maclean'll be desperate to finish him off.'

'I will, will I?'

I spun round with a sick feeling that had nothing to do with the pitch and roll of the ship. Maclean was standing in the entry to the cabin, and I was in Syd's arms. It was too late for pretence.

'I see you know my cabin boy's little secret,' Maclean said to Syd, taking a step into the canvas-sided room.

My friend flushed with anger and his grip on me tightened.

'If so,' Maclean continued, 'you'll know that I hold her life in my hands; one wrong word from you and I'll give her up to the captain's justice.' He spoke confidently but his eyes were shifty, watching Syd's every move warily. He was clearly less than pleased that I had so formidable a protector.

'Justice?' growled Syd. 'If there was any justice on this ship, you'd be in irons.'

'That's mutinous talk, man.'

'No, it's the truth, but it ain't no surprise that you don't recognize it,' Syd spat contemptuously.

Wow, Syd, I thought, impressed by my friend's comeback.

'Understand this, Maclean, if you lay another finger on Cat, or Frank for that matter, then you'll 'ave me to answer to. You won't 'ave a chance to run to the captain, so you can stop bleatin' about that.'

'Threaten all you like, but you know there's nothing you can do to stop me.' Maclean seized my arm and yanked me away from Syd. 'What are you going to do now, eh? Thump me? If you do, you'll be locked up and well out of the way for many days for hitting a superior. Just think what I can do in that time. You certainly won't see your sweetheart again.'

Syd was quivering with rage, his fists balled. Maclean grinned and put his arm none too gently around my neck.

'Good, I see you understand. Now get lost. I don't want you within six feet of my little cabin boy. Got that?'

Syd swung his arm.

'Syd!' I shrieked, pushing against Maclean so that he stumbled back out of range. The punch missed – just. 'Don't, please! For my sake!'

With a great effort at self-control, Syd turned on his heel and left the cabin.

'Glad you know your own interest, my dear,' chuckled Maclean. He released the grip on my neck. 'Keep your friends in order and you at least might survive this voyage.'

Blown to within fifty miles of the coast of America, well off course, the *Courageous* did not look very brave after the storm. When the winds finally dropped, the deck had been so battered it looked as if it had been on the receiving end of the enemy's broadside. The foremast was an ugly stump, our remaining sails in shreds. The first job was to get her back into a condition to limp to shore and this was why I found myself doing the last thing I expected.

'Sewing!' I groaned, sitting cross-legged with Pedro as we repaired what appeared an acre of canvas.

'Chance for you to shine then, Cat,' Pedro remarked as he made beautiful neat stitches up his side of the tear. 'All those lessons with Mrs Reid finally come into their own.'

'You forget, my son, that I was the one chucked out of the wardrobe department for my complete lack of skill with the needle.' I threaded the twine through the blunt instrument I'd been given and attacked my side of the problem. 'I don't know what it is about me and sewing; we will never be good friends, I fear.'

'Ssh!' Pedro nodded to where the captain was striding among the men. Barton was a sight in his patched uniform, lace dangling from his sleeves like a hound's slobber. If anyone needed the attention of a good needlewoman, it was him, but he appeared not to notice his own slide into slovenliness. He approached our little sail party and stopped just behind Pedro.

'Excellent, my lad!' said Captain Barton, patting his favourite on the head, treating him rather too much like a dog for my liking. He turned to my efforts. 'Ah, it's you. So, you thieving rascal, show me what you've done.'

It appeared that he wasn't ever going to let me forget that accusation; I was marked as a bad lot. I held up my patch of canvas for inspection. It looked all right to me, much neater than my usual.

'Can you do nothing right, boy? You're mending a sail, not embroidering a lady's petticoat! If you carry on making tiny stitches like that we'll be here until doomsday. Mr Lely!'

The first lieutenant bobbed up at the captain's side immediately. 'Sir?'

'See this boy gets extra practice at sewing.'

'Aye, captain.'

My emotions had all been in a scramble since the terrible night of the storm. I almost burst into a fit of insane giggles. All my employers had taken this view of my handiwork, but for very different reasons. Too clumsy for the wardrobe; too fine for the sea. Of course, I bit back my laughter: far too dangerous to risk any show of emotion near the captain, let alone something that could be construed as disrespect.

The captain strode off and Pedro finally dared meet my eye. He said nothing, just raised an eyebrow.

'Don't say it, Pedro!' I warned him, knowing full well what he was thinking.

He grinned. 'I was just wondering what Mrs Reid will say when I tell her that you were accused of doing too dainty stitches.'

'She won't believe you,' I said flatly, setting to with more freedom now I had been ordered to speed up. The stitches were big but tight. Was this what was wanted?

'No, I agree. It is far more incredible than the story of how you came to be sewing sails in the first place.'

Mr Lely paced back to inspect our progress. A heavy hand patted my shoulder.

'That's more like it, lad,' the first lieutenant said. 'We'll make an able seaman of you yet.'

I felt a warm glow in the pit of my stomach, a feeling that had long been a stranger to me: satisfaction.

'Thank you, sir.'

'Carry on, carry on. The captain said to practise.'

'Yes, sir.'

Mr Lely strode off, hands clasped behind his back. I paused to thread my needle again, waiting till he was out of earshot.

'That does it,' I whispered.

'Does what?' asked Pedro.

'If I'm getting extra sewing as a punishment, I'm definitely jumping ship.'

Pedro began to chuckle. 'You endure the hold, storms, false accusations, half rations and I know not what, but it's sewing that finally breaks you?'

'Too right. It was the needle that broke this camel's back.'

After the battering we had taken, the *Courageous* had to reach landfall before we could make ourselves fit for open sea again. Most pressing was the need to replace our water: ten barrels had been damaged during the storm when the foremast came down. The captain also wanted to replace the lost mast, which meant finding a tree of sufficient size to rig up in its place. All of this meant one thing.

'It has to be Georgia,' declared Mr Lely to Belsize as the two walked the main deck where I was sewing yet more sail. They didn't notice the small person practically buried under the swathes of canvas. Pedro had gone with the rest of the men to collect their grog, but as I was on half rations, I would not get mine until the evening. No loss in my opinion: I still hadn't taken to the stuff.

'M-must we go to America, sir? Can't we make it back to Bermuda?' asked the junior officer, scanning the horizon suspiciously.

Lely shook his head. 'You know I do not always see eye to eye with a certain person,' he said and they both looked instinctively up to the quarter-deck, 'but I agree with him in this. We have to risk rebel shores or risk dying of thirst.'

Belsize tapped his hands on his sides nervously. 'A-at least we're no longer at war – th-that's one good thing.'

Lely paused and drew Belsize into the shadow of the stairs, the older man standing protectively over his young colleague.

'That would be true – in any other ship.' He looked furtively around, speaking in a whisper. 'But our illustrious captain earned himself something of a reputation during the war. The Yankees still clamour for him to be handed over to answer for his crimes. If they find out he's replenishing the ship on their territory, they'll descend on us in force.'

Belsize's inexperience showed in his shocked reaction. 'B-but he's an officer in the king's navy – th-they wouldn't do that!'

Lely gave a hollow laugh. 'Are you so sure, Belsize? You're too young to have served in the war, but these are still the same rebellious American colonists we are talking about. You expect them to respect the envoy of the king they rejected, especially a man responsible for a massacre of American civilians?'

I shivered, burrowing down into the sail cloth: I sensed that I was about to learn more than I wished about the demons that pursued our captain.

'S-so it's true then, sir? He did order the savages to pillage that man N-North's estate?' asked Belsize.

Lely dropped his voice another notch; I bent forward to listen. 'Yes – though the captain told us then that he saw North as a leader of the revolutionaries and a threat to British rule. He thought the man's family and loyal slaves were fair game too.'

'What happened?'

Lely stood up and curled his lip in distaste. 'He managed to persuade the rest of the slaves to turn on the family by bribing them with a promise of freedom. So Barton and his crew attacked at dawn with a party of Creek Indians. With the help of the slaves he'd bribed, they killed the whites and any loyal blacks that tried to defend the family, then retreated to the ship. A miserable business and it achieved nothing but bloodshed.'

'So the f-family were k-killed by their own servants?' wondered Belsize aghast.

'Slaves, lieutenant, not servants. If you keep men like beasts, you should not be surprised when they turn and savage you. You can't blame them really – the black slaves, I mean: by all reports, North was a cruel master.'

Belsize rubbed his hands in a nervous gesture. 'B-b-but still, they betrayed their own master!'

'In the hope of something better. For them,

Captain Barton was their only chance of freedom; the proud boast of American independence was never going to extend to slaves. Still, the Yankees have never forgotten that day: they've mercilessly pursued those involved in the attack and I can tell you now that they'd be very pleased to get their hands on Barton to punish him for what he did.'

Belsize coughed as if he could already feel the halter at his neck. 'S-so is it really wise to go ashore on American soil?'

Lely smiled, his gaunt features lighting up for a rare moment. 'There's a little place I remember – an island. The fort's been abandoned for some years but the mooring's still good. It's very out of the way so the captain has decided to risk it.' He gave a mirthless chuckle. 'Of course, we'll all be in trouble if the American navy get wind of our presence. I imagine the captain will order extra gun training in anticipation of an engagement with the old enemy.'

'And the inhabitants of the island?'

'Friendly in the main. And the fort? Only the Creek Indians go there these days.'

Belsize gave a whistle. 'You're a g-genius, sir. They're probably the only people in America that would give us a w-welcome.'

'I didn't say they'd welcome us. Their brief cooperation with the captain was some time ago. But I think we stand a better chance there than anywhere else within five days' sail.'

SCENE 3 – FORT FREDERICA

My mind was now made up to leave the *Courageous*, come what may, but I wondered how to make my farewells. Syd and Frank would try to stop me so it was best they knew nothing. I did not want to risk them accompanying me in case they were recaptured. With one flogging apiece already on this voyage, I did not want to guess what Barton would see as a fitting penalty for two runaways. Desertion was punishable by death. Even Pedro might baulk at the idea of me going alone and argue that he should come too. But I wasn't about to lead my friend into a country where, as I had just heard, his fellow Africans laboured under the cruel yoke of slavery. It was dangerous enough for me; for him – well, let us say that I judged it much safer that he stayed with Frank in the hope that my absence provided a chance for the truth to emerge.

So I decided to say nothing to any of them,

though I was tempted every moment to break my resolution.

We were bound for the abandoned fort on St Simon's Island at the mouth of the Frederica River. It commanded a good position on a bend of the river, which would give the crew warning of any unwelcome visitors in the shape of George Washington's navy. I could see the fort's outline on the horizon as we approached, the walls oddly geometric against the untidy wilderness of scrub and forest that surrounded it. Harkness, a veteran of the American war, told me that the fort had once stood at the head of a settlement with neat houses laid out in straight lines. After a fire, the place had been left to disappear back into the sandy margins and the villagers had long since gone. Now the *Courageous* dropped anchor a short distance from the rotting jetty – a short distance that could be swum, if a girl knew how to swim, that is.

This girl doesn't. Not much call for swimming in Drury Lane. I knew the theory: thrash your arms and legs about and try not to drown, but I preferred not to put it to the test. Fortunately for my plans, Maclean had to go ashore to supervise the refilling of the water casks and he decided it was safer to take me with him.

Maclean and I had barely spoken since that terrible night during the storm. Our messmates could not fail to notice something was even more wrong than usual and I'm sure our presence cast a shadow over each meal. Mrs Foster put it all down to my 'master' still being angry about my 'pilfering' from the stores and, kind soul that she was, decided that it was high time we made our peace. With this in mind, she approached me as we loaded the casks into the boats and took me aside.

'Looking forward to putting your feet on dry land, Jimmy?' she asked, giving me a friendly squeeze around the shoulders.

'Yes, ma'am.'

'Be a good boy and I'm sure your master will come round,' she said in an undertone, pressing a little parcel into my hand.

'What's this?' I asked in surprise.

'Oat cakes. Made them myself with the last of my stock. They're for your dinner.'

'Thank you.'

'You see, you do not have to steal to receive good things, Jimmy.'

'I know, ma'am.'

She tutted and shook her head. 'Your master may seem harsh but he has to be cruel to be kind. Boys have to be curbed.'

It pained me that Mrs Foster thought me a thief. Then again, she also thought me a boy so everything about our relationship was false.

'I'm not bad, Mrs Foster. Whatever Mr Maclean says to you, please believe me: I just want to do what's right.'

She chuckled and hugged me closer. 'I never said you were bad, Jimmy. A young'un's stomach takes a lot of filling and it's a sore temptation to be down in the hold surrounded by victuals, perhaps only a saint could withhold his hand from taking a quick sample. But we have to resist, especially on board a ship like this. You know that now, I hope?'

I nodded, then felt my ear pulled.

'Excuse me, Mrs Foster, but the boy has work to

do.' Maclean was on my back the moment he saw me having a half decent time.

'I know, Mr Maclean,' she said primly. 'I was just having a quiet word.'

'Well, less of that, if you don't mind. You mustn't spoil him by kindness.'

Mrs Foster folded her arms over her generous chest. 'A young lad needs sunshine as well as showers, Mr Maclean. Too much cruelty pushes them away.'

'I thank you for not interfering,' snapped the purser, propelling me towards the boats. 'He's my business, not yours.'

'More's the pity!' she called after us. 'Bye, Jimmy!'

I saluted, thinking it was the last I'd probably see of my kind protector. Maclean grunted angrily and shoved me towards the rope ladder. Once down, I huddled in the bow of a boat as the rest of the landing party climbed in. I could see my other friends going about their business: Syd was watching me from the yardarm. I gave him a nod to signal that all was well. Frank was leaning on a mop, chatting to another sailor, unaware that he was missing my departure. Pedro was perched on a coil of rope on the main deck, tuning his violin – the captain had ordered a concert that evening and he'd been given time to practise. It seemed a strange way to take my leave. I wondered whether I would see any of them again. And now I had no time to say any of the things I wanted: how much I cared for all of them, how much I admired each and every one of them.

'Goodbye,' I murmured to my friend, the buxom figurehead, as the rowers strained on the oars. 'And God speed.'

My first step on American soil was not auspicious: my foot passed right through a piece of rotten planking as I clambered out to tie up the boat. The fragments splashed into the water below but I managed to stay dry. Looking about me I took in some deep breaths of fresh air. It was a cold day: if Spring did come earlier in these southern climes then it was taking its time. The grass on the shore had a tired dark green hue, the trees were still bare and a chill wind whipped up the river from the sea bearing spits of rain. Most of what I saw was familiar from home, but then an unexpected note would emerge: an exotic tree with thick spiky leaves, strangely shaped crab shells picked clean by long-necked white birds. It was both familiar and foreign at the same time. I began to wonder if it was such a bright idea to jump ship after all.

'Stop gawping, boy, and do some work!' grumbled Maclean. He glanced nervously over his shoulder towards the treeline.

'What's the matter, Mr Maclean?' asked Harkness, putting his shoulder to a barrel to roll it to the stream. 'What are you afraid of: ghosts, Indians or Yankees?'

'Or all three,' quipped a sailor in a red cap.

'Hold your tongue!' Maclean glared at the man and pushed me ahead of him.

Harkness sidled up to me as we wrestled the barrels into a deep clear stretch of the stream.

'You know what's eating your master, don't you, Jimmy?'

I shook my head. To tell you the truth I wasn't

bothered about Maclean; I was thinking about how to make my escape.

'You'd better know or you'll only get into more trouble. He was with him, you know,' continued Harkness in an undertone.

'With whom?'

'Barton – on the North raid. Surely you heard the whispers about that?'

I nodded.

'Maclean was the captain's agent with the Indians. He's almost as popular with the Yankees as our beloved leader.'

Yes, that fitted somehow. Civilization sat ill with Maclean: I could imagine him relishing a bit of murder and pillage with the red-skinned men. All the stories I'd ever heard of the Indians bore witness to their savagery and violence. If they were friends of his, they were the last people I wanted to meet right now.

'Lovely man,' I said sardonically. 'Aren't I just the luckiest lad alive to have him as my master?'

Harkness chuckled. 'It could be worse.'

'Could it?'

He noted my serious tone. 'Aw, Jimmy, nothing lasts for ever.'

No, it doesn't. Particularly not if you stop dithering, Cat, and get on with what you know you have to do, I told myself.

Our barrel successfully filled, I waded ashore. All this running water had given me an idea.

'Sir,' I said meekly, tugging at Maclean's shirt, 'I need a moment to myself.'

'No,' he said sharply.

'I really need a moment, sir,' I said more urgently, hopping from leg to leg. 'Please!' I leant forward and whispered, 'It's woman's stuff; I have to do something about it or they'll notice.'

Maclean blushed (as I knew he would) and pushed me away. 'Go on then. Get lost.'

'Thank you, sir.' I intended to follow his order to the letter.

I turned away from the party at the stream to look for the nearest cover. The trees thickened the further you got from the fort; that would make hard going but it also offered the best hiding place. I headed up the sandy shore for a hundred yards, then clambered up a bank held together with a mass of tree roots. With a final glance behind – Maclean was still watching – I disappeared into the trees.

For the first time, I was really alone. The further I went, the more distant my old life seemed. The cobbled streets and pavements of London, the glitter and shallow glamour of the theatre, the carriages and horses: these were dropping over the horizon as I sailed into these new seas. All I had were the clothes I stood up in and some oat cakes. I was terrified but determined.

You probably know me well enough by now, Reader, to understand that if there's one thing Drury Lane has not prepared me for it's the wilderness. I can cope with the wildlife on the streets of London, the entanglements and snares laid by my fellow Britons, but this vast untamed place was beyond me. I thought I'd become familiar with the countryside at Boxton but now I realized that Frank's estate had more in common with Hyde Park than with this forest. It was a labyrinth, guarded doubtless by monsters large and small. Shrill calls of birds overhead made me jump, twisted roots and thorny plants tripped me up. As I walked on, I tried to make it feel less strange by dredging up the Shakespearean poetry I knew about the wild, but rather unhelpfully all that would come to mind was the famous stage direction from *The Winter's Tale*: 'Exit stage left chased by a bear.' Were there bears? I had no idea. There were certainly snakes – Harkness had already warned me when we were in the stream – but I trusted to luck to keep these out of my way.

One monster would definitely be on the hunt. Maclean would come after me, I had no doubt. Without his hostage, his position on the *Courageous* was very precarious. If anyone believed Frank, then the purser was dead meat. His trap, which seemed so impregnable while on board with me under his thumb, looked very flimsy once I removed myself from the picture. I didn't have long to make good my escape. Recapture was not an option that bore thinking about.

This realization propelled me onwards. I began to stumble, half running through the trees. It seemed to matter little if I lost my way; I didn't really know where I was in any case. I just needed somewhere to evade Maclean until the ship sailed. Trusting to Barton's desire to get away from America as soon as possible, I guessed that meant only a few days at most.

A few days!

In that case, I would need shelter and, ideally, a way off the island. I turned towards the shore. Perhaps it would be possible to wade across to the mainland at low tide? Or maybe there would be a fisherman or a passing whaler?

Emerging on to the beach several miles north of where I had started, I saw that the further shore was still as far off as ever. No wading, or even swimming. After all that thrashing through the undergrowth, I decided I'd earned myself a short rest and a bite to eat while I thought what to do next. Lying down in the sandy dune, hidden by the long grass, I broke open Mrs Foster's present. The oat cakes tasted wonderful, reminding me that I'd not eaten anything freshly baked for many weeks. I took one – saving the rest for later. As I lay chewing, head resting on my elbow, the sun struggled out from behind the grey clouds, transforming the dull shore with its magic touch. The warmth from the sun was quick to make itself felt on my back. More comfortable now, I realized that it really was quite beautiful here. And, after all, city girl though I am, I could still appreciate the feel of the sand under my fingers, the whisper of the wind in the grasses. I closed my eyes, slowed my breathing, trying to disappear into my surroundings.

I could do this. I would find a way to reach Lizzie and Johnny in Philadelphia, my name would be cleared of all suspicion and I could don a dress again.

Mind you, I quite liked breeches.

It was the splash of a stone hitting the water that woke me from my daydream. I raised my head cautiously and scanned the shoreline. Not far up the beach, someone was walking slowly in the shallows, pulling on a string behind them. Expert fingers inspected the catch dangling from the bait, bagging a lusty crab with glee and throwing back a tiddler. Then the line was cast out again – the little stone weights pulling it below the surface.

I sank back down and gulped. I'd wanted a fisherman – and I'd got a fishergirl. But what was wrong was that she was a red-skinned one. Images of tomahawk-waving savages flashed through my mind. I glanced at her waist, wondering if she would have a row of scalps dangling by their hair, but her belt held nothing but a pouch and a knife.

A knife.

Call me a coward, but I decided to retreat into the woods. My scalp was not going to be anyone's trophy if I had anything to do with it. I tried to step as lightly as possible but a twig snapped as I backed away. The girl raised her head; I sank down; her gaze travelled past me. With a sigh of relief, I saw her return to her work.

Back in the cover of the trees, I pondered my near encounter. She hadn't looked warlike but I had heard nothing but horror stories about the native people of this land. All things considered, I'd done the right thing not to approach her. But if she was here, that probably meant there were others. And where there were people, there would be boats. If I followed her and waited until nightfall, perhaps I could 'borrow' one – all right, steal one – and make my way to the mainland.

I spent the rest of the day shadowing the fishing girl. She turned back north as the evening approached and walked along the beach, swinging her catch of crabs in a large pouch. I could tell she was happy from snatches of hummed songs that reached me in the trees. I wished I felt so carefree, but what with fear of her and anxiety that Maclean would catch up with me, I had probably never felt less like singing.

Rounding a spit of land, the girl disappeared from view. I scrambled after her, slinking through the trees and climbing over obstacles as fast as I could, desperate not to lose my ticket off this island. I had to come down on to the shore to wade across a stream, but then I reached the point she had rounded. Cautiously, I peeked out from behind a bush to see what lay beyond. I had been right: three canoes were beached in a bay. The girl was now running towards some dark-haired men building a campfire. They waved as she approached. One scooped her up into a hug –

Family. She seemed to be talking excitedly. The tallest man glanced in my direction but then looked over his shoulder into the trees at the back of the beach. Did they suspect something? If they did, they did nothing about it, choosing instead to unpack the girl's bag and admire her collection of crabs. Perhaps she was just telling them about her good day's work? I certainly hoped so.

I made my way through the trees as silently as I could, keeping the flickering light of the fire in sight to guide me. I decided to lie in wait until they slept, praying that they would feel safe enough to set no guard. Finding a fallen trunk to hide behind, I hunkered down. With only the beetles and buzzing insects for company, I couldn't help but feel envious of the girl at the campfire. Shouts and laughter reached me – they were having something of a party, it seemed. I hoped it wouldn't mean that they were planning on a late night. I feared I would drop off to sleep before I got my chance.

I wasn't going to fall asleep.

Absolutely not.

I did.

SCENE 4 – SAVAGES

It was the middle of the night when I woke. A fly was buzzing in my ear and the annoyance had brought me to my senses. Creeping forward, I took the risk of approaching the campfire. I could still see the glow, but it looked as if it had been allowed to burn down to the embers. There seemed to be four dark bundles lying in a circle around it: the girl and her three friends, asleep, I guessed. Giving them a wide berth, I dropped on to the beach near the boats. The canoes had been drawn well out of the water behind a large rock. Glancing towards the sleepers, I tiptoed to the nearest vessel. Several leather-wrapped bundles lay on the bottom. Savages though the Indians were, I felt bad enough about stealing one of their canoes; I wasn't about to take their stuff too. As quietly as possible, I lifted their belongings out and placed them carefully on the sand.

Thwack! A blow caught me on the side of the

face, sending me spinning into the river. I gasped, taking a mouthful of water, then panicked. The Indians may have caught me but I was determined not to be taken alive! My attempt to wade deeper into the river was thwarted by a hand grabbing me by the top of the head and dragging me back to the beach.

'Found you!' crowed Maclean triumphantly. He shook me until my teeth rattled, then threw me to the ground. 'You are coming back with me, but not before I've taught you a lesson!'

I didn't know what scared me more: the murderous look in the purser's eye as he grappled for his whip or the fear that he would wake the sleepers.

'Indians!' I gasped, scrabbling away on my hands and feet.

Maclean was too intent on his revenge to take any notice. He swung the cat-o'nine-tails; I twisted like a snake; the ends bit the sand.

'Stay still and take your punishment!' he shouted.

Terrified, I backed away until I hit the rock. Covering my head with my hands, I waited for the blow to fall.

It didn't come. A pebble clattered at my feet. I looked up to see Maclean shaking his hand in agony. A tall, thin man with two long black braids stepped out of the shadows.

'Put it down,' he said in halting English, pointing at the whip.

Two more men appeared at his side – behind them the girl, this time swinging a catapult, looking mightily pleased with herself.

Maclean took a step backwards and held up his hands, the whip drooping in his numbed grip.

'I am friend of the Creeks,' he declared. 'You see him; the boy was trying to steal your boat. Let me punish him.'

The leader turned to look at me cowering at the foot of the rock. After my ducking in the river, my hair was straggling over my face and my clothes were soaked.

'It is girl,' the Indian said simply, not fooled by my disguise.

'Ye-es, but she was stealing from you nonetheless,' said Maclean with a gesture towards the canoe.

'We watch. She took things out. We not know what she want.'

'It's clear enough, isn't it? She was going to steal a boat and run to the mainland.' Maclean's fists curled. This delay did not suit his fiery nature at all. 'She's wicked – evil – an outcast of her people. Leave her to me.'

I had no intention of being in Maclean's power ever again. I made a rapid decision, praying my choice was sound.

'Please, don't hand me over to him,' I begged the Indian on my knees. 'I'm sorry about the boat. I was just trying to get away from him.'

The Indian approached and raised me from the ground, keeping a strong grip on my elbow. He touched my cheek with his fingertips. I flinched. Maclean's blow had given me another bruise to add to my collection.

'Come to fire. We talk.'

He towed me along in his wake and directed me to sit down on one of the heaps of blankets – decoys, I now realized, to make me think they were all asleep. The Indians must have known about me for some time but waited until I made my move before deciding if my intentions were hostile. That gave me hope that they were not going to do anything rash in revenge for my attempt to steal a boat. I was thankful they had given me the benefit of the doubt; I wouldn't have stood a chance against all four of them.

The girl threw some more wood on the fire as the leader looked again at my cheek. He said something in his own language to the older of the other two men. Much to Maclean's disgust, this man drew out a pot of ointment from his pocket and gently rubbed it on the bruise. Satisfied, the leader sat down and crossed his legs. The others took positions around the fire, the girl immediately opposite me where I could see her dark eyes glittering in the firelight. They waited.

Maclean was the first to break the silence. He had obviously been working out what he was going to say during the brief interlude. He turned to the leader.

'Honoured sir, as I said, I am an old friend of the Creeks. This girl is my kin; I claim her.

She must return with me to my ship.'

The leader ignored the latter part of this speech. '*Old friend?* Creeks have no old friends among white men.'

Maclean gave a snort. 'Your fathers will remember me, young man. I am Maclean, agent of Captain Barton.'

From the looks of consternation that passed round the little group, I guessed that this name was well known but not welcome.

'We remember Captain Barton,' acknowledged the leader. 'I am Tecumseh. My father knew him.'

Maclean nodded. 'Then he also knew me. I am pleased to meet you, Tecumseh – a fine son of a fine man.'

I was sinking further into low spirits. If Maclean got all pally with these Creeks I was done for one way or another. I clutched my knees to my chest, waiting for the next move.

'This is my . . .' Tecumseh searched for the English word, 'uncle, Killbuck.' He nodded at the older man who had put the balm on my bruise. He was a head shorter than his nephew and his hair was shot through with silver. 'And this is my brother and sister, Little Turtle and Kanawha.'

Little Turtle was a stocky young man with a stubborn jaw, a complete contrast to his willowy brother and sister. I could see how he might have earned his name for there was something hard-shelled about him. I guessed he would be a tenacious fighter. Kanawha most closely resembled Tecumseh: slender and handsome with her brown eyes and long dark hair worn loose. She bore herself with elegant poise, or at least that's what I would have said if this had been a London ball-room and not the savage shore of America. Here 'elegant' did not seem to fit.

Maclean bowed to the listeners, clearly believing himself on the home straight.

'I am honoured to sit at your fireside, friends. But sadly I cannot stay, for my ship sails and I must return before dawn. I will take the girl and leave you in peace.' He cast a triumphant glance at me. I lowered my head to my knees, plumbing new depths of despair. In the silence, the wind picked up, rustling the leaves and making the fire flare. A spark spat out at my feet, catching light on dry sea grass. I ground it out with my heel, thinking all hope extinguished.

But then it happened.

'We are sad to lose our friend Mac Clan, but the girl does not have to go with you,' said Tecumseh levelly.

Maclean drew a sharp intake of breath. 'But she is mine, I tell you.'

Tecumseh shook his head slightly. 'No. When since do white men enslave white women? Is she your wife? She is too young for Mac Clan. You claim you are kin, but what kinsman would treat his kinswoman as you treat her? If she were your dog, I would let her free.'

I couldn't believe my ears, nor could Maclean from the expression on his face. Livid didn't cover the half of it.

'No, you can't . . . I have to take her back with me . . . I demand that you give her to me!' He rose abruptly but Little Turtle slid between us, blocking his path. Maclean turned back to Tecumseh. 'By what right do you keep her? I am your friend; she is your enemy!'

The girl broke into a peal of laughter. 'Enemy? She is no threat to us – she moves through trees like a herd of buffalo!' She stomped her feet on the ground in imitation of my attempts to pass unheard.

'Enough, Kanawha,' interrupted Tecumseh. He turned to me. 'Girl, what is your name?'

'Cat,' I said in a whisper.

'And, *Cat*,' he said the name hesitantly, 'is this man your kinsman?'

'No, sir.'

'Do you wish to go with him?'

I shook my head fervently.

'There: that is clear. Friend Mac Clan go back to his ship; Girl Cat stay here.' The other three nodded their agreement.

Maclean was having none of it. 'No!' He turned to the older man, Killbuck. 'You, sir, speak to your nephew: for the sake of our past friendship, the Creek people owe me this much.'

Killbuck had a strange expression as he looked back at the purser. 'I remember our past dealings with Mac Clan. Friendships die. Regrets come. We have no friends now.'

Maclean was struggling to control his temper. 'If I can get no justice from you, I will speak to your chief then. Where is he?'

'Chief of the Wind Clan is not far,' said Tecumseh, refusing to be ruffled by the slur on his judgement. 'We take you to him.'

Maclean gave a groan of frustration, clearly wondering how long he could afford to stay away from the *Courageous*. 'Can we leave now? See him at once?'

Tecumseh nodded. 'We leave now. *Vhoyvkets!*' The Indians rose as one and swiftly broke camp, stowing their gear and scattering the ashes; soon there was no sign they had ever been there. Tecumseh approached and put a hand on my shoulder, gazing into my face with his calm dark eyes. I felt my fear ebb away. I knew who the savage was now and it wasn't Tecumseh. 'Girl Cat, you travel in my canoe.'

I nodded, grateful that he wasn't making me ride with Maclean.

The girl dodged round the purser and grabbed my arm. 'Come, I show you.'

The three Indian men pushed the boats out into the shallows. The canoes were made from hollowed logs that could be either poled or paddled, depending on the river. Maclean clambered in with Killbuck; Kanawha helped me into the biggest canoe while her brother steadied it. They then turned for the mainland and began paddling across the water. They bent and dipped the oars in rhythm as if they were moving in time to a song I couldn't hear.

I shivered, still dazed by my changing fortunes. A blanket was draped over my shoulders from behind.

'Thank you, *Kanawha*,' I said, trying the name out on my tongue. It tasted strange – a language I had no handle upon, slipping out of my control.

She chuckled, amused by my clumsy pronunciation.

A thought then struck me. 'Mr Tecumseh, sir?'

The Indian raised the paddle. Water ran down the edge of the blade, dripping like quicksilver into the water. 'Yes, Girl Cat?'

'When you said the chief was near, how near did you mean?'

Tecumseh smiled. 'Two days upstream.'

Maclean wasn't going to like that; no, not one little bit.

The fireworks began at dawn when Maclean realized that we were still heading up the Frederica River with no sign of nearing an Indian settlement.

'Put us ashore!' he bellowed at Killbuck. 'I'm taking the girl back right now!'

Killbuck continued to paddle as if nothing was happening.

'Tecumseh, I'm warning you!' shouted Maclean across the water. 'You take me to the *Courageous* or you and your people will suffer the consequences!'

The young leader's face remained impassive: he too was temporarily deaf.

Maclean then turned his attention to me. 'You little witch! I'll kill you when I lay my hands on you.'

Taking a leaf out of my hosts' book, I feigned

inscrutable composure – something that was much easier to do knowing there was a safe stretch of water between us. This drove Maclean over the edge. He lunged for the paddle and tried to wrestle it from Killbuck. All he received in return was a stunning blow to his head which knocked him back. He lay flat in the bottom of the boat, mouth still gaping at the shock that anyone might stand up to him.

Tecumseh said something to his sister. She laughed.

'Why are you laughing?' I asked, wondering if I could risk making conversation.

Kanawha sought for the words to translate. 'Brother say, "What a peaceful morning now we enjoy."'

I smiled to myself. Yes, peace at last.

Maclean sat up some minutes after the tussle clutching his head, but he must have decided his best course of action was to bide his time. I could feel his gaze like the heat of a fire on the back of my neck. He blamed me for this abduction, which was wonderfully ironic if you think about it. Despite worrying about my own fate, it was pleasant to reflect that he was getting a taste of his own medicine.

The day passed slowly as the three canoes made their way upstream, leaving arrow-shaped wakes as we plunged into the heart of this mysterious world. I passed the time gazing at the banks, trying to understand what I was seeing. I knew we were on the edge of a vast land, still barely known to white men. The forest seemed to stretch for ever; there were no landmarks that I could discern, no taverns or milestones, every stroke of the paddle taking me farther from home. How did the Indians find their way?

Kanawha had been watching me and interpreted my interest in line with her own.

'There, good hunting,' she said, pointing to a tangle of trees. '*Weleetka*. River good to fish. A happy place.'

I nodded. It felt the polite thing to do, as one would when a gentleman shows you the features of his estate. 'Very . . . er . . . pleasant. Does it belong to your family?'

She shrugged. 'Yes, that is what white men say. They give us rolls of paper saying ours but then return and take it away. I do not understand how it is ours if it is theirs also.'

I frowned. 'But if the land is yours, by law they can't take it. You should throw them out.'

Tecumseh, who had been listening to our conversation, nodded. 'You are wise girl, Cat. You should be Indian.'

I felt a hand pull at my pigtail: it was Kanawha playing with my ginger hair, perhaps checking it was real. Her gesture reminded me that I was still dressed like a boy and no longer needed to keep up the disguise.

'Can I borrow a comb?' I asked.

She felt in her pouch and pulled one out. 'I do it.'

Tugging off the string that had confined my hair, she let it fall free in straggling locks. She lifted an end and sniffed.

'What is on it?'

'A kind of grease – the sailors use it to keep their hair back.' Maclean always insisted that I kept it under control so that no girly locks escaped.

'Smells like whale.'

'Probably is.'

'Yuck.'

It did little for my self-esteem to be repulsive to people I had thought of as savages until a few hours ago. The canoe lay low in the water. The answer was obvious.

'Excuse me a moment.'

I dipped my head into the river, making the canoe lurch. Kanawha shrieked and Tecumseh pulled me back.

'You spill us out,' he scolded. 'Sit still. We stop soon.'

With cold water dripping down my neck, I watched as Tecumseh angled the canoe to the shore. We reached the little beach before the other boats. Kanawha skipped out, beckoning me to follow.

'Quick,' she called, 'before Mac Clan gets here. We go wash. Brothers cook breakfast.'

I ran after her. She led me some way into the trees until we reached a little stream that fed into a stony pool. It was icy cold but I didn't care.

Stripping off my filthy sailor's clothes, I plunged in. Kanawha dug in her pouch and threw me a bar of rough soap.

'Come in: the water's lovely,' I lied, splashing her.

Laughing, she shook her head and backed away.

Once I had seen to myself, I turned my attention to my clothes. Rubbing with soap and beating them on the stones, I soon had them reasonably clean. The only problem now was that they were soaking wet. I began reluctantly to clamber back into them, shuddering at the unpleasant feel of wet cloth on my skin.

'No, no. You die of cold,' said Kanwaha seriously. 'Wait here.'

She disappeared and after ten shivering minutes she returned from the camp bearing a pile of clothes. 'These are mine. They fit you.'

The folded garments smelt a little of fish but were soft and dry. I pulled on a long green cotton blouse with a wide cape collar edged with silver coin brooches, somewhat like a gypsy's shawl. The garment fell to my knees and was belted with a cloth appliqué tie, decorated with beads. I then stepped into a pair of black buckskin leggings edged with red. They felt comfortable and warm – so much better than petticoats or the ragged trousers I'd been wearing. Proud of my colourful new clothes, I held out my arms.

'How do I look?'

Kanawha covered her mouth with her hand to laugh. 'You are like Indian maid now.' She took the comb out and attacked the tangles in my hair. 'Now I plait.'

By the time she had finished I was completely transformed into a pale-skinned, red-haired Indian with hair bound back by a beaded ribbon.

'Cat of the Cat Clan,' she dubbed me, tapping my tattoo, which peeped out of the scooped neck of my tunic.

I bowed. 'Greetings, Kanawha of the Wind Clan,' I said formally.

'Breakfast?' she suggested.

'Race you?'

And with shrieks of laughter we bounded through the trees like two deer with Spring fever.

She won of course.

*

Back on the river, I was enjoying being a passenger. My fate had been placed in the hands of others and I could do nothing. Accepting this, I let go of the fear that had burdened me for so long. Every hour Maclean spent trying to get me back gave Frank a chance to prove himself. I had achieved what I intended and it no longer mattered what became of me. I had no sense that these particular Creeks were planning to do any of the terrible things I'd read about. If anything, they were going out of their way to be friendly. All in all, for someone adrift in an alien land, I judged I wasn't doing too badly.

Kanawha passed the time in the boat telling me stories of her people. Every sight and sound seemed to cue another legend, full of the creatures and scenery of this country. She told me how the Indians believed that the land was created by Crawfish, who stirred up the bottom of the sea so that mud came to the surface. Next, Buzzard flapped his wings and made it dry, forming hills and valleys. Then came Light, creeping at first into the world thanks to Star. Moon soon followed and finally Sun. When a drop of blood fell to earth, the first people sprang up in that place. That was certainly something I'd never heard mentioned in church on Sundays, but then my parish priest had told me we came from a garden, shaped by God from the dust, His breath in our bodies, so perhaps our beliefs were not so very different after all.

Sitting silently in the canoe as we travelled further into the unknown, drinking in story after story, I felt that Kanawha's words were spinning a magic spell around me. The stories fitted this world, slipping into place like a foot into a well-worn shoe. My old life seemed so far away, as unreal now as this country had been to me when I'd heard travellers' tales in London. Nothing that mattered to me there made any sense here. What was Drury Lane to a girl who knew nothing of plays and acting? Would Kanawha not find the idea more alien than any of her legends were to me?

As the riverbanks flowed by, Kanawha told yet more stories about how her people had learnt to hunt, to grow corn, and how they were taught to live in balance with the world they knew.

Until the white men.

When they came, many of her people were killed by the pox until the Indians were weakened, unable to hold on to what was theirs. Now they were continually being made to move on, dwindling into the woods or going west.

I couldn't help feeling ashamed of my skin as she spoke. To her, we were the wily tricksters who bully when strong, lie when weak.

'You must hate us,' I commented after she had told me of yet another betrayal by my kind.

Kanawha looked surprised at the suggestion. 'It is . . . complicated. Some of us have married with white people. We learn to speak your tongue.'

'But we hate those that kill, lie and steal,' Tecumseh butted in from the other end of the canoe.

I gulped: had he been thinking of my attempt to liberate a canoe from their possession?

'Now there are so few of us, some hunt among other tribes in the mourning wars,' he continued.

'What are mourning wars?'

'When we lose our brothers we go and seek new blood. We capture prisoners to take their place, people to become one of us.' He whistled over to his brother in the third canoe, summoning him alongside. 'Tell Girl Cat how many you brought back last time you went hunting.'

The hard-shelled warrior Little Turtle smiled at me and held up five fingers, mistaking my shocked expression for admiration. 'Two got away,' he admitted with a modest shrug. 'We let them go – they were not worthy.'

My throat was strangely dry. 'And what if the prisoners don't want to join your clan?'

'They have no choice,' Little Turtle said dismissively as if this was not a consideration.

'I see.'

I turned back to Tecumseh and saw that he was looking at me with particular intent. Suddenly Kanawha's gifts of clothes bore another, very disconcerting meaning.

'But I suppose it's just other Indians who you recruit, isn't it?' My voice was almost a squeak.

Tecumseh shook his head. I think he was

laughing at me. 'No, if someone is meant to be one of us, it does not matter where they come from. Our leader, Chief McGillivray, had a Scottish father, his mother was half French. Only a quarter of his blood is Wind Clan. He is well chosen to be our chief in these times, do you not think, when our future depends on how we deal with strangers?'

'Er, yes, I suppose,' I muttered, wondering where this was leading.

'And with hair like yours, you could be one of his children.'

I kept quiet, thinking no answer was safest.

Kanawha leant forward and tied a shell necklace around my throat. A moment before it would have been welcome; now I felt unsettlingly like a favourite pet being pampered. I fingered the tiny shells, completely at a loss as to what I should do.

'You said captives have no choice. What did you mean exactly?' I asked Little Turtle.

The warrior steered skilfully around a rock poking out of the water like a shark's fin and rejoined us on the far side.

'Captives are either killed, enslaved, or adopted,' he replied.

'And how do you decide?'

'The clan decides. It depends what we need.'

'And at the moment, what do you need?'

Little Turtle grinned. 'I do not know. We have been away long time.'

'So have I,' I muttered, thinking of the months that had passed since I had been at home among the theatre people who knew me. I missed Drury Lane, the streets around Covent Garden, the sense of belonging somewhere. I had never seriously considered that I might not return; now this truth struck me like a slap to the face. I had leapt out of the frying pan, and now found myself in the fire.

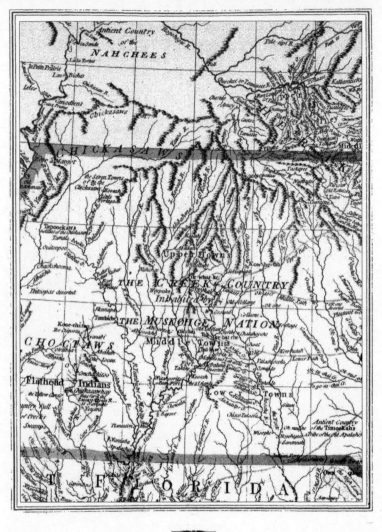

Act IV — In which a horse
breaks Cat in . . .

ACT IV

SCENE 1 – WIND CLAN

Towards dusk at the end of the second day, we paddled up to a landing stage and disembarked. Scores of other boats were tied to the wooden jetty, bumping gently into the supports as the river current tried to entice them away. Racks of nets were stretched out to dry, the rank smell of fish powerful on the night breeze. Tube-shaped fish traps made from hoops covered in hide were stacked neatly on the quayside. A hundred yards or so away, lights twinkled among the trees.

'Home, Chickamauga,' said Kanawha, shouldering her bundle. 'Come.'

She led me up a well-trodden path away from the clouds of little insects that hummed on the margins of the river. Having nothing to carry, I took a bag of crabs from Tecumseh and followed. The creatures were still alive, squirming desperately in the sack as if they knew their days were numbered. Kanawha had promised me a crab stew fit for kings, a speciality of her grandmother, so I had a vested interest in lending a hand. She had already reached the trees. I sped up to catch her as Killbuck's canoe was now at the mooring. I could hear Maclean cursing and complaining. He was intending to have the business settled immediately – this night or never, as he'd declared to me only that morning. Even though the *Courageous* would probably have sailed by now, Maclean pinned his hopes on returning to the nearest seaport and finding a trading schooner to take us to the West Indies to catch up with it.

I had argued with him, telling him he wasn't thinking straight. The chances were that it was already too late for him to restart the charade of me being his cabin boy. He'd not taken my cool reasoning well and vowed that I was going with him or going to hell.

That's what he thought.

Kanawha took my arm and pulled me through a rickety gate and into a kitchen garden. At the far end of the path was a little cottage built from wood and thatched with reeds. I was surprised. I did not know what I was expecting – tents or caves even, not this: this looked so familiar. I suppose I had never imagined the Indians' home, thinking they were permanently on the move, huntsmen not farmers. Indian furs were famous and much sought after in the fashionable world so I had assumed that the trappers lived wandering lives on the trail of big game. My education had clearly been faulty: there was more to Indian life than beaver skins, as proved by the fields of newly sown crops that surrounded the village.

'Like it?' Kanawha asked hopefully, pointing to the cottage. 'It is Grandmother's house.'

'Yes, I like it.'

As Kanawha ran down the path, a huge dog burst from round the back and rushed to her, leaping up with both paws on her shoulders, smothering her face with licks. To my nervous eyes, the beast looked more wolf than dog. She danced with him for a moment, before taking his collar.

Kanawha said something in her language, then

repeated it for my benefit in English. 'Yopo, this is Cat. *Enhesse*. Friend.'

I approached gingerly.

'Hold out your hand so he can smell you,' Kanawha ordered.

I did as I was told, trying not to flinch back as the great hound sniffed my scent.

'There, he know you are friend now.' Kanawha let go of his collar and bounded to the front door. '*Puse! Puse! Estonko!*'

A high shriek, like the sound made when the fox gets in the henhouse, echoed from the hut. Decked in a red tiered dress with colourful appliqué edging and a profusion of bead necklaces, a tiny woman rushed on to the porch, arms outstretched.

'Kanawha, *heres ce!*'

The little lady folded her granddaughter in a hug, then held her out at arm's length, checking her over to make sure all was well. Her white hair hung in two thin plaits either side of her beaming face. With skin as wrinkled as dried prunes and only a few teeth remaining, she looked to me at least a hundred years old. Kanawha whispered something then nudged her grandmother to look in my direction. Not knowing what to do, I curtseyed when I saw the old lady's dark eyes were upon me. This provoked a peal of laughter that would have cracked the bells of St Paul's.

'Come,' she chuckled. 'Welcome.' As I moved within reach, she clutched my forearm, pinching the skin. Turning to Kanawha, she spoke rapidly in her own tongue.

'My *puse* does not speak many words in your language,' Kanawha explained. 'She thinks you look too pale – like a ghost.'

I shook my head, meeting the woman's gaze. 'I'm no ghost, Grandmother.'

With a cluck of her tongue, she patted my cheek hard and beckoned me to follow her into the house. I guessed this meant she was now convinced I was flesh and blood.

The house was furnished simply – table, chairs, a low bed with a quilted cover – but everything was spotless and smelt of fresh herbs. It was the first comfortable place I had been in since Boxton and

I could not help sighing with relief as I sank into a chair – before immediately leaping to my feet again as a cat yowled and shot away. The old lady cackled with laughter as she pushed me back down. Kanawha was already putting a cauldron of water on the hearth – she had been serious about her promise of stew. The two Creek women chattered away in their own language and, from the occasional glances thrown in my direction, I guessed that my predicament formed part of the general catch-up. The cat, by now recovered from her shock, leapt lightly on to my lap and I stroked her, soothing both herself and me. If I'd learnt anything it was to grab my peaceful moments when and where I could.

'Come, eat,' said the old lady.

I woke with a start. I must've drifted off to sleep. A delicious smell filled the kitchen.

'Excuse me, Puss,' I apologized to the purring cat as I hoisted her off my lap.

We had all just sat down to table when a tall youth with a high forehead appeared at the door.

He said something, nodding his head curtly at me. I put my spoon down, feeling a heavy dread that my peace was at an end, but my hostess was not about to waste good, hot food. She shrieked at the young man, letting loose a barrage of rapid, angry words, completing the performance by driving him from the door with a broom. She then returned to the table, smiling contentedly.

'Eat, eat!' she said, waving her hands at me like a goose-girl herding her charges to the trough.

I was not one to disobey such a formidable personage. I glanced at Kanawha to see she was grinning proudly at her grandmother.

'What did she say to him?' I whispered.

'She told him to take his lazy bones on to the porch and wait for us to finish. Even the chief cannot order Puse Fo about.' Kanawha swallowed a large mouthful of stew and patted her grandmother's arm appreciatively.

'Puse Fo?' I queried.

'Grandmother Bee — little but with a terrible sting, no?'

Thanks to Grandmother Bee, I had ample time

to finish my stew before the second messenger arrived, asking where we were. This time the broom stayed in the corner and it was me that the old lady ushered out.

Kanawha took my arm as we followed the two messengers down the path. The newcomer appeared to be teasing the other for being scared of the little woman's displeasure, but the boy who had felt the edge of Puse Fo's tongue was having none of it. I didn't need to speak their language to understand that he was saying: 'I'd've liked to see you stand up to her.'

'Where are we going?' I asked Kanawha as we passed rows of cottages like Grandmother's.

'To the chief's house. He owns lots of plantations around these parts – this is just a small one.'

Small, she called it! I had thought Indians were all about loincloths no bigger than a duster and makeshift forest camps, waving tomahawks and yelling war cries. Shows you how much I knew – and how wrong were those so-called travellers who regaled us with such tales. Imagine it, Reader: a white-boarded house at the end of the trail, fine enough for a rich merchant. A broad porch ran around the house, many people standing or squatting in its shelter awaiting an audience with the great man. Everyone was decently, if eclectically clad, in a mixture of European and Indian styles. Not a hint of war-paint or an axe in sight. It could have been any high-born man's doorstep in London – the same collection of petitioners: debtors begging a reprieve, creditors calling for settlement of their account, people after favours. The fact that they all bore the tanned skin of the American Indian did not change the essential familiarity of the scene.

Our guides led us straight inside. It was only here that I knew we really were in an Indian rather than European house. The walls were decorated with brightly woven tapestries, some depicting the creatures of Kanawha's tales. Rush mats covered the floors; spears, shields and other weapons hung above the fireplaces. By the front door, a tall, almost life-size, carving of a warrior wearing a mask snarled at all incomers. I could hear the sound of a child crying in the distance and a woman hushing it with a lullaby. A black servant passed us, carrying a tray of empty glasses. Not a servant – a slave. It hadn't occurred to me until that moment that the Indians would also own African slaves: I'd thought of the original inhabitants of this country as the underdogs, but I now I saw that even underdogs have underdogs. I was relieved I'd left Pedro behind.

'Go in,' said the first guide, gesturing to a room to the right of the main entrance. 'They wait for you long while.'

From his tone, I could tell that satisfying my hunger had probably not been wise. But there was no choice to undo what had happened. I stepped into the room, grateful to have Kanawha at my shoulder. It took a moment for them to notice us standing irresolute by the door, giving me time to take in the scene. A group of some twenty or so Indian men were seated in a circle, Killbuck and Little Turtle among them. Maclean was sitting on a low chair at the left hand of the chief, speaking fast and chopping at the air to emphasize his words. On the right sat Tecumseh, but he was very still, deep in his own thoughts. As for the chief, what first struck me was what a strange mixture of Indian and European he was. His hook-nosed face and pale skin would not have seemed out of place in the streets of my home except for a certain – how can I put it? – immobility in his features, inherited, I suppose, from his Indian mother. It gave him an imposing air as if he was above the low passions that swayed most men. His hair was long and streaked with grey. He wore a tailed jacket and shirt over soft leather trousers; a brightly coloured sash of beads hung from his shoulder to his waist. Despite the splendour of his appearance, he did not look in good health: grey shadows haunted his eyes and lingered in the hollows of his cheeks.

'So, you see, sir,' Maclean was saying, 'the girl has to come back with me. If she doesn't, my captain will be very displeased and I'm sure McGillivray of the Wind Clan does not want to be at odds with Captain Barton of His Majesty's navy. One girl is not much to buy peace.'

The liar! Captain Barton did not know I existed, much less care what became of me. If Maclean had any sense, he would have long since given up any idea of rejoining the ship – his stratagem had failed once I gave him the slip. But it appeared he was not throwing in the towel yet. I feared all that he wanted now was revenge and I would never leave this forest alive if I went with him.

McGillivray now raised his eyes, noticed me standing by the door and beckoned me forward. The Chief's gaze was cold – no comfort for me there then. Kanawha pushed me gently in the back and I took a few paces to come just within the circle opposite him.

'Girl Cat, what is this man to you?' the chief asked quietly.

At least he was interested in my side of the story.

I took a breath, trying to calm the torrent of accusations that were queuing up to spill out. 'An enemy. On the orders of his master, he abducted me and my friends, sir. He tried to kill one of them, a rich young man, son of an English noble, but he didn't manage it.'

'Lies,' growled Maclean. 'This little trollop was running away to sea after her lover. I'm to take her back to her father – he's a great friend, a good man. I wouldn't want to see the family shamed.'

'Is this true?' asked McGillivray.

I shook my head. 'I've never had a father; in fact, I have no parents at all.'

McGillivray looked at me in silence for some time, his fingers arched together, lips touching the tips. I guessed that as a man surrounded by enemies – American settlers to the north, Spanish and French to the south, other tribes on all sides – he was well used to weighing up what would be most advantageous to his people. He must be skilled at it if the wealth of this house was much to go by.

'Sit,' he ordered at length. 'I have heard something of you from Tecumseh. He says you have travelled far to escape this man. Tell us about yourself.'

About myself? I sat cross-legged on the carpet and pondered my answer. How could I make the most of this chance to win over this audience? No one seemed to like Maclean much so maybe they would be readier to believe me? I noticed Little Turtle on my right watching me closely; he smiled slightly as if to encourage me.

'It is a long story. What would you like to hear first, sir?' I asked.

Chief McGillivray settled back and closed his eyes, his face drawn. 'Tell me of your home,' he replied in a distant voice.

'London?'

'Yes, I have heard many marvellous tales of that place, home to the king who was once my chief.'

I glanced around the circle of men, all waiting expectantly. Well, if I wanted to win the hearts of the Creek people, I should do it in a language that was familiar to them. I remembered how Kanawha had told me the history of her people, not as a list of names, dates and places, but as a series of animal stories. That gave me my cue.

'Then let me tell you the story,' I began, 'of how the wily sparrow stole a diamond from under the nose of the greedy shepherd boy. Once upon a time, there lived a sparrow at the top of one of the tallest buildings in the great city of London far, far over the seas . . .'

A murmur of approval ran round the circle. Tecumseh's eyes brightened, Little Turtle nodded and McGillivray himself sat up. Maclean tried to interrupt but the chief threatened him in no uncertain terms with ejection.

I continued, warming to my theme as I turned my friends into the creatures of Kanawha's myths. I imagined Pedro as a black hare, capering madly on stage; Frank was transformed into a raven; Syd took shape as a bull, pawing the earth angrily as his domain was threatened; I darted in and out as the sparrow.

McGillivray ordered refreshments to be handed round and signalled to me to continue.

Coming to the matter at hand, I told how the half-tailed fox – I cast a dirty look at Maclean – had plucked the raven from his roost and run away with him to sea, taking the hare and sparrow too. The fox threatened to kill the little bird with a snap of his jaws or turn her over to the wolves if the raven and hare did not do his will. But the sparrow had taken flight one day, flying into the unknown to draw the fox away from her friends. Now she had landed here and knew not what would become of her, but at least the raven and the hare were free. She would not lead them back into the trap set by the fox, for all his growling and nipping at her heels.

A chuckle followed this remark. A bowl of tobacco was passed around the circle, pipes filled. Soon I was sitting in a smoky fog worthy of any gentlemen's club in St James.

'You are clever, Girl Cat,' said the chief at last, resettling his sash across his chest. 'Cleverer than Maclean here.'

'What!' spluttered the purser.

McGillivray ignored him. 'He comes among us with shallow friendship and weak threats, forgetting we have more reason to hate than love him. We have suffered for his actions on behalf of that man Barton. But you, you come with nothing but yet give us a treasure of stories to win us over.' He sucked on his pipe stem, the tobacco glowing red for a moment. He expelled a wisp of smoke. 'How old are you?'

'I'm not sure, sir.'

'You cannot be more than fourteen summers, maybe less.' He tapped the bowl of his pipe thoughtfully. 'So wise so young. Perhaps it is not natural. Are you a witch?'

'No!' I protested.

Maclean leapt on the word. 'That she is, sir. Don't listen to her or she'll get you under her spell.'

A mutter ran round the room. Some of the eyes that had been friendly but a moment ago were now looking at me with hostility.

McGillivray gave me a sour smile. 'Oh, we were all under her spell, I have no doubt about it. But what to do with her – and you – that's another matter completely. I will sleep on it.' He turned to me. 'You can go; but send no nightmares to haunt me. I cannot be swayed by any witchcraft of yours.' He looked back at Maclean. 'And issue no more threats: they do not impress me. You are a man of crooked tongue, Maclean, as you have ever been.'

With that, we were both dismissed. I hurried away as fast as I could to keep out of Maclean's reach. Kanawha had to run to catch up. As soon as she was in earshot, I blurted out over my shoulder: 'I'm not a witch! I'm not!'

I was more distressed by the accusation than I cared to reveal in that gathering. I knew that in our enlightened age I shouldn't believe in witches but the age-old fears seemed particularly powerful in this wild place. For all I knew, they still burned witches at the stake. I had thought I was being clever, trying to fit my world into theirs; instead, I had only called down yet more suspicion on my head. Was I always destined to be in the wrong?

'Cat is upset?' asked Kanawha in confusion.

'Too right she is,' I muttered.

'But witch is not always bad. Grandmother is one too, our *heles-hayv*, our medicine maker. She makes good medicine for us. Your stories are good medicine.'

I paused at the gate, collapsing against it after my dash across the village.

'Oh, Kanawha, what do you think is going to happen?' I felt at the end of my tether. 'If I were a witch, I wish I could really magic myself into the sparrow and fly home.'

'I think,' she said, taking my arm in hers, 'that now we go to bed and sleep. You can do nothing; Mac Clan can do nothing tonight.'

She was right: it was out of our hands.

The next morning Grandmother Bee turned us out of our blankets at dawn. She had three split-cane baskets carried by a buckskin strap across the chest and a knife for each of us.

Kanawha sighed. 'Come on, Girl Cat. There is work to do.'

We staggered blearily after the old lady and out into the dew-damp of the early morning. The earth smelt rich; you could almost hear the plants stirring after their winter sleep, roots thrusting a path through the soil. Then the birds began their performance, starting with a lone voice singing its aria in a bush, then second soprano swooping in, closely followed by third. The song built until a whole host was competing to dominate the territory. Some cries were so shrill they seemed to shred the air.

'What are we doing?' I yawned.

'Collecting for medicines,' Kanawha explained. 'Try not to stray. The forest is full of swamps, very dangerous if you do not know the land.'

Resolving to keep close to my guides, I walked in Kanawha's footsteps as we pushed our way into the woodland. Near the village, trees were sparse, many having been felled for building materials and firewood, but further in the wild took over. We walked among pines and magnolia just beginning to bud. We passed under woody vines that spread from trunk to trunk like green-fringed shawls, and through clusters of trees I'd never seen before and could not name. Beard-like moss drooped from oak trees, transforming them into giant old men standing still as statues. Startling green ferns sprang up from fallen trunks, snapping open like a coquette's fan at a ball at the touch of Spring sunshine. It was all so foreign, so bewildering, so beautiful.

From time to time, Grandmother Bee would stop and cut something, signalling us to do the same; a root or a bulb, a fresh leaf or dried berry – all were thrown into our baskets. I could see that

Kanawha was fretting, bored with this work as I had so often been with darning at Drury Lane. That made me smile, but I was just relieved to be doing something that didn't involve climbing a thirty-foot mast.

Towards midday, we approached a part of the forest where the ground was stagnant and shifted underfoot. Cypress and cane grew in thick clumps in muddy water. Midges hummed in the air, feasting on my freckled skin as if they had never seen anything so delicious. Seeing my discomfort, Grandmother rubbed me with an ointment she carried in a pouch at her side. Now able to look about me without the constant attention of the flies, I spotted a crop of bright red flowers in the distance.

'What are they?' I asked, taking a step towards them.

Kanawha caught the back of my tunic as my foot went ankle-deep into the mud.

'*Opelika* – big swamp,' she said. 'And they are a warning – only grow here.'

'Thanks for telling me.' I sat down and emptied

the water out of my shoe. It was certainly good to be with someone who knew her way around.

We were released from our botanical duties after noon. Kanawha was in a hurry to return home, leading me back to Chickamauga at a punishing speed.

'What's the rush?' I asked, wiping the sweat from my brow. Though it was early spring, I was finding this land of Georgia hot and stuffy in the middle of the day; it must be nearly unbearable in high summer. A more complete contrast to the cool drizzly weather of London I could not imagine.

'Brothers are breaking in new horses,' she said excitedly. 'They let us ride if we get there in time.'

'Oh.' The memory of my experience of riding side-saddle at Boxton came to mind. I had hardly coped with a docile mare; unbroken horses were definitely not for me.

Kanawha jogged out from the trees to a paddock at the edge of the village. Tecumseh and Little Turtle were already there, leaning against a fence as they watched three horses cropping the grass a few yards away. They were smaller than horses I was used to in London, not built for heavy work or pulling a cart, but they looked tough enough for riding. One was a piebald with a scraggy black mane, the other two were a lovely honey colour.

The two men looked up as we approached. Little Turtle made space for me to lean beside him. Tecumseh pointed to the trio of horses.

'Magnificent, do you not agree, Girl Cat?' he said.

I nodded. 'Yes, they're lovely.'

'White man brought many curses with him when he came to our land, but one blessing followed him: our brother, the horse.'

'Where did you get them?'

'The chief bought them in Florida from a Spanish officer.'

Kanawha interrupted us, chatting away in her language. Her brother shook his head, replying in English.

'Only the piebald is broken; the other two are as wild as the day they were born.'

'I ride, yes?' she asked eagerly.

Tecumseh thought for a moment, then held out a bridle. 'If you are careful. I do not want to be stung by Puse Fo for getting your head broken. Sasakwa is still nervous.'

Little Turtle snorted and shook his head dubiously.

I waited next to him as we watched Kanawha walk slowly towards the piebald. The mare stared at her, nostrils flaring in suspicion. The Indian girl held out her palm, allowing the horse to smell it. Next she laid a hand on Sasakwa's neck, talking in a low, melodic voice. All was well until she produced the bridle: Sasakwa was off like the wind to the other end of the paddock.

Little Turtle laughed. 'She does not like you, sister.'

Kanawha frowned and marched back to her brothers, throwing the bridle on the ground.

'You said she was broken in,' she muttered angrily to Tecumseh.

'I said she was nervous. She has been running from us all morning. She does not like us either.'

Tecumseh turned to me. 'What about our little witch: do you have a way with horses as you do words?'

'I'm not a witch,' I grumbled, 'and no, I absolutely do not have a way with animals – I've only ridden a few times and very badly.'

Little Turtle glanced at his brother then picked up the bridle and passed it to me. 'Show us,' he coaxed.

'It'll be a waste of time.'

He just smiled in that unflappable way of his. I took the bridle, intrigued by the two brothers' patience. From what Tecumseh had said to Kanawha, they had been at this all morning and failed to get anywhere. Most English horse-breakers would have been in the paddock with a whip and spurs by now, forcing the horses to submit. The Indian brothers appeared unruffled, content to feel their way to a solution.

'I might as well give it a try then.' I jumped the fence and walked slowly towards the horses. The two honey coats galloped away as soon as they spotted me; the piebald tried to stare me out as she had Kanawha. Close to, she seemed much bigger than she had from the other side of the fence – all muscled limbs and hooves. Her smell brought to mind the sensation of falling from the grey at Boxton – not the landing but the feeling just before I parted company with the creature – a sense of being completely out of control. I glanced over my shoulder, hoping I wasn't about to lose face in front of my new friends. Perhaps it didn't matter because they couldn't hear what I was saying. I held out the bridle.

'Right, you mean old thing, I don't want you to take a step nearer. Just make it look as if I'm trying, all right?' I jiggled the bridle. 'That's right: keep on staring at me like that. I'll give it a few more seconds then give you up for a bad lot.' I held out my hand as Kanawha had done. 'There, you're not going to cooperate, are you? That's fine by me . . . no!'

I smothered a yelp as the horse trotted forward and lipped my fingers. I swear that she was eyeing me mischievously, fully aware of the panic inside me.

'Good!' called Tecumseh. 'Forget the bridle. Try lying across her back – get her used to the weight of a rider.'

'You can't be serious,' I muttered.

If I was reluctant, Sasakwa certainly wasn't. She moved alongside and gave me a disdainful look.

'You're a tricky one, aren't you?' I muttered as I stroked her neck. 'Flirting with us, playing hard to get.' I reached over her back, wondering just how I was going to get up. 'You're only letting me do this because you know I don't want to.'

The mare snorted and shifted her hooves.

Taking that as a final challenge, I jumped and used my arms to lever myself up so that my head was hanging over one side, my legs the other. Sasakwa began at once to trot, bumping me up and down like a sack of meal on the miller's pony. After ten paces, the inevitable happened and I slid off, ending up sitting in a pile of recent manure.

Breaking her in? You must be joking: she was totally in control of this.

Little Turtle ran to my side and helped me up.

'Good. I had theory, I was right,' he said, very pleased with himself.

'Theory?' I stared grimly at the mare who was watching me from a few paces away.

'Sasakwa was broken by a Scotsman in Florida. I think red hair reminds her of him and tells her who is master.'

Yes, she knew full well who was master, but it wasn't me.

'Try again. This time I'll help you sit on her back.'

'No, really, I think I've had enough –'

'No, no, now is time to build on your success.' He dragged me over to the fiendish mare, who stood waiting good as gold. The little coquette.

'Ready?' Little Turtle seized my waist.

'But there's no saddle!' I protested.

'We do not use a saddle,' he replied, hoisting me astride the creature.

I grabbed a fistful of mane. Sasakwa tossed her head and began to trot again; I could feel myself sliding all over her back. I gripped with my knees. It was easier than side-saddle; at least I was in touch with what the beast was trying to do: she was trying to unseat me.

'Oh no, you don't,' I muttered.

She began to buck, throwing me forward. I lurched to grab a hold round her neck, by no means in charge of the situation, but at least I hadn't been dislodged. Sensing she wasn't going to get rid of her limpet that way, Sasakwa sidled into the fence, squeezing my leg against the top bar. I was angry now; she was a vicious little thing and I was blowed if I was going to let her get the better of me. I clung on, gritting my teeth. Next she tried a gallop across the field; that almost proved the end of me, but anyone who has clung to the shrouds in a gale is well trained to keep hold on to a horse. Finally, she slowed to a trot and bent forward nonchalantly to crop the grass, as if nothing had happened. That undid me. I slid forward and ended up lying on the ground, staring up into her mouth. She snickered and lipped me again, her teeth knocking my forehead. As she hadn't taken the chance to trample me, I think that meant we were friends.

I think.

SCENE 2 – ADOPTION

My afternoon of being broken in by Sasakwa turned out to be time well spent. When Tecumseh reported my 'success' to the chief, it helped swing the clan's opinion in my favour. I was to stay, at least until the horse was properly trained. And that, Reader, promised to be a very long time indeed for that devil of a pony.

When the verdict was announced that evening at the chief's house, I expected the purser to explode. But he didn't: Maclean just nodded his head once and left the room. That put me on my guard immediately – it was so out of character. I would have preferred it if he had cursed and raved as that would have been a sign of his frustration. He left the village the very next day, promising me that he never wanted to lay eyes on my miserable face again. The feeling was mutual but it seemed too good to be true. Was I really so easily rid of him? I hardly dared believe it, but he was indisputably gone, last seen heading downstream for a trading post.

The other person who seemed less than happy with the decision to keep me on as horse breaker was Kanawha – not that I was staying, but that I had been given the task she wanted. She watched me leave each morning with undisguised resentment as all she had to look forward to was another day of plant collection. I would have loved to swap the bruises I was gathering for her basket of herbs, but no one would hear of it.

Four days into the horse training, Grandmother Bee came to watch. She stood with Tecumseh at the edge of the paddock, a little figure in a vivid red shawl, shielding her eyes against the sun's glare. Sasakwa had decided that my lesson for the day was to learn how to take humiliation. She allowed me on to her back now but only so that she could dump me with greater effect in front of my audience. Grandmother found this highly amusing. She said something to Tecumseh, tapped his arm, then disappeared into the forest.

I groaned, wondering how much more of this my poor bones could take. Tecumseh helped me to my feet.

'What did she say?' I asked as I hobbled on his arm to the fence. The pony smirked at me from the far end of the paddock, chewing a mouthful of grass.

'Grandmother say that Sasakwa is your spirit sister.'

'What does that mean?'

'She is stubborn and does not do what she is told. With blood like that she will be a good breeding stock – make our herd strong.'

I let go of Tecumseh's arm. 'I'm sure she will. Perhaps you should get someone else to ride her now. I think I'm only teaching her bad habits.'

He shook his head. 'No, our chief say that only you will do.' He smiled and patted my shoulder. He had kind eyes, deep brown like his sister. 'You are happy here, Girl Cat?'

I wondered at the change of subject. 'Happy enough, though I worry about my friends.'

'But you have new friends here?' His eyes narrowed.

'Yes, I suppose I do, but as soon as I can, I want to find my old ones. They're like family to me; I belong with them. In fact, two of them live in Philadelphia. I don't suppose there's a coach or even a boat that I could take to reach them?'

Tecumseh laughed and pointed to the north into the forest. 'Philadelphia: that is far, far away. I have never been half that distance. Even if you found a vessel to take you, you would still need a lot of money to buy a passage and it would take many weeks.'

'And if I walked?' I asked hopefully, encouraged that he had at least heard of the place.

'Impossible. There are thousands of rivers and many mountains between us. You would not manage that journey.'

I groaned in disappointment. The vastness of America was something I had heard much about but now, for the first time, it struck home. I couldn't just jump in a carriage or on to a barge to get to my destination in a few days or weeks as I had been able to in England and France; I was trapped by the wilderness. A wave of panic swept over me.

'Come,' said Tecumseh, patting my back consolingly. 'Let us teach Sasakwa to respect her rider.'

I clenched my fists, trying to get a grip on my emotions. There was no point in giving in to my fears; I could not afford to show weakness if I was to survive. Far better to concentrate on the task at hand and earn my freedom by completing Sasakwa's training.

With Tecumseh's help, I was able to remain in contact with the pony's back for the rest of the session. In my own humble estimation, I was beginning to get the feel for riding and no longer sat rigid with terror anticipating disaster. I even began to enjoy it.

'We made progress,' Tecumseh noted as we left the paddock. 'You will be a rider yet.'

'Why not?' I said, filled with the optimism of the amateur. 'After all, I've been a dancer and a sailor – why not a horsewoman too? Frank always said I could be whatever I wanted.' I felt that now familiar pang of homesickness again: where was Frank now? Had he and Syd kept Pedro safe in Jamaica, out of his old master's hands – if that was where they were by now? And had he been able to persuade someone that he was the son of the Duke of Avon?

Observing my change in mood, Tecumseh put an arm around my shoulders. 'Do not worry, Girl Cat: you will not feel that you are a stranger forever. You will soon feel at home.'

I didn't want to feel at home: I wanted to *be* at home. The Wind Clan was a fine family, but it wasn't mine and never would be. I tried to put this into words.

'I'm sorry, Tecumseh, but I'll never fit in here. I'm like . . . like a bird that is just passing through on its passage from one country to another.'

He shook his head. 'No, you nest here now. I will speak to our chief and Grandmother. We will make you one of us and then you will no longer pine for things you cannot have.'

I reached the cottage still mulling over what

Tecumseh had said and found Kanawha practising with her bow. She had been cool towards me the last few days, but seeing me so unhappy seemed to melt her mood.

'Come, Cat, you must learn how to hunt,' she called from the field behind the house. She had set up a target: a flour sack strung from a pole, and was hitting it faultlessly despite its pendulum motion. I was impressed.

'Now you try.'

She handed me the bow, showing me where to hold it, how to fit the arrow to the string, the movement needed to pull it back. It was far tougher than I had imagined. I loosed a shot – the arrow ploughed into the earth well short of the target. Kanawha broke into a peal of laughter.

'Again!' she said, scooping the arrow up. 'I will keep the target still for you. Remember, think about how the arrow flies.' She sketched a graceful arc in the sky. 'Aim higher.'

The next arrow fell from the string before I even had a chance to release it. The third disappeared into Grandmother Bee's vegetable patch, provoking a squawk of indignation from the hens that were rooting for grubs. On my fourth attempt, the arrow sailed past the target, far too high. Kanawha charitably took that as a sign of improvement.

I put the bow aside. 'I'm pretty useless, aren't I?'

'Yes, you are,' she agreed, rather pleased by this discovery.

'And you're so good at everything: fishing, hunting, running.'

'Yes, I am.' Kanawha stretched her arms above her head, flexing her strong, capable muscles. 'But this was how I was raised. You must be able to do something that I cannot. What were you taught?'

Indeed, what had I learned in my hand-to-mouth existence backstage at Drury Lane? Not much that made any sense here.

'I can read and write.'

She shrugged.

'Speak Latin.'

'What's that?'

I didn't think it worth the trouble to explain it

was a language no living civilization spoke. What else could I do?

'That's about it really,' I admitted.

She looked disappointed, and I felt I had let Drury Lane down with my utter failure to impress her. But the swinging target gave me an idea.

'No, no, wait. I can do this.'

I had spent months last year training as a ballerina; it might just make an impression on Kanawha. I ran to the fence, hopped out of my shoes, and began to warm up.

'What are you doing?' Kanawha asked.

I grinned. 'You'll see.'

Once prepared, I climbed on to the fence, gained my balance – easy when you've practised up a mast with a thirty-foot drop below – and began a series of ballet steps, moving fluidly through the positions, rising to tiptoe. I admit, Reader, standing on the beam was unnecessary but I was showing off. I didn't think Kanawha would be astounded by my skill unless I made it more dramatic.

'What is that?' she wondered, staring at my feet.

'Try it, it's harder than it looks.' Humming the tune I had danced to in the Paris Opera, I pirouetted on the beam. Kanawha attempted to copy me but ended up tumbling from the fence.

'See? I told you it was hard.' I leapt down lightly and helped her up. 'That is something called ballet – a sort of tribal dance we perform back home. People come to big houses and watch us do it.'

She frowned, trying to comprehend the world I was describing. 'Why?'

'Because it is beautiful – because they enjoy it – I don't know – many reasons.' Explaining made me feel foreign again.

This time with feet on the ground, Kanawha repeated the moves clumsily. She would need a lot of practice if she wanted a job in the chorus line.

'You should dance at the ceremony,' she said.

'What ceremony?' I corrected her posture as my teachers had so often done for me.

'Your adoption. The chief has decided you are to become one of the Wind Clan.'

I froze. 'What!'

'Yes, it was settled this afternoon.' Kanawha abandoned the ballet with a shrug and took up archery again, eyes fixed on the target rather than my shocked face. 'It is good news, no? It means Mac Clan can never take you away.' The arrow flew from her fingers and hit the target spot on.

Good news? Not for me. I had always wanted a family, but it had never occurred to me that it might consist of Indians in a remote part of America.

'But will you let me leave after that?' I asked, squeezing my feet back into my worn shoes. 'Will I be free to come and go as I wish?'

A second arrow pierced the swinging sack in the centre. She lowered the bow. 'You will not be a prisoner, Cat, but once you are married you must stay with your husband.'

'Married!' This was getting worse and worse.

'Of course. I am to be married to McGillivray's son at the Green Corn Festival and someone has already asked for your hand. We can be betrothed at the same time.' She smiled at me, clearly expecting me to be pleased.

I appeared to be the last person in Chickamauga to know the plans for my future happiness.

'And do I get any say in the matter? Who wants to marry me?' I took up a stick and beat the fence in frustration.

Kanawha was surprised by my reaction. For an Indian girl, marriage was the event they all looked forward to; she really thought she was the bearer of glad tidings. 'My brother,' she said tentatively, trying to work out what was wrong as I lashed the gate. 'You do not like him?'

I paused in my whipping, taken aback. Tecumseh wanted to marry me? He was very handsome – I was flattered despite myself – but he had not shown the least sign of romantic feelings towards me in the time we had spent alone together.

'Of course I like Tecumseh.'

Kanawha laughed. 'No, no, not him. He is to marry the chief's daughter. No, I am speaking of Little Turtle. Tecumseh suggested you would be a good match for him as he is too shy to ask one of the village girls. You will be his first wife.'

Wonderful: I was to get the bashful little brother – the one named after a creature normally made into soup – rather than the tall, dark and handsome leader.

Not that I wanted to marry anyone.

Aargh!

I took a deep breath and gathered up the fragments of stick that had borne the brunt of my frustration. Kanawha was looking at me as if I had gone mad.

'What is wrong, Cat?' She seemed genuinely upset that I was not ecstatic.

'Everything.' I slumped to the ground and threw bits of wood disconsolately at the hens that had the ill judgement to come near me. 'I'm really grateful to you all but I don't belong here. I'm Cat Royal from Drury Lane, London. I don't want to stay here: I want to go home.'

Even to myself I sounded like a whining child asking for the moon. How was I going to go home? I was stuck in the middle of nowhere with no money or prospect of getting away. These kind people were making me part of their community and I was being ungracious. I hadn't forgotten that the other two options for captives Tecumseh mentioned had been death or slavery – I had got away lightly.

Kanawha took the remaining sticks from my hands and squeezed my arm. 'After tonight, your past will be behind you. Little Turtle will make you a wonderful life partner: he is kind and generous. You are very fortunate.' She said the last words wistfully – I wondered why.

'And your young man: what is he like?'

She grimaced. 'Too old. Not so kind. But it is a good match for my family. I am content. He will be away often on his father's business. His other wives are friendly.'

I swallowed a protest at the mention of multiple wives.

'Why marry him if you don't like him?'

'I am content,' Kanawha repeated, signalling that the conversation was at an end.

That evening I was led to the village meeting place – a space in the centre of the settlement marked by a circle of poles. All the clan had gathered, a fire had been lit in the middle and everyone was talking and laughing. Feeling like a cow led to the shambles, I allowed myself to be walked three times round the outer edge of the ring, then guided to the feet of the chief. Gentle pressure on my shoulder indicated I should kneel. My heart thumped desperately: I wanted to run but there was nowhere to go. I had no choice but to let this happen.

An exchange took place in the Creek language as Tecumseh petitioned the chief to allow me to join the tribe.

'*Enka, enka!*' chanted the chief. He bent forward and kissed my forehead. 'Welcome, daughter.' He placed a string of beads around my neck.

I bowed in acknowledgement, hands on my thighs as Kanawha had taught me.

'Rise, Cat of the Wind Clan,' announced the chief, bringing me to my feet. He led me three times round the tallest pole – the totem of the clan, carved with the creatures of their tales, guardians of the village. After the final circuit, he placed my hand in Tecumseh's as the eldest male in

Kanawha's family. 'Look after your sister,' McGillivray told him. 'She is now your kindred.'

Tecumseh bowed.

My adoption complete, the celebrations began. Musicians processed into the ring, Little Turtle was chief among them, proudly beating on a set of drums. His eyes sparkled when he saw me watching him. I looked away, aware that we had not yet broached the subject of my unwillingness to wed. A group of young men leapt into the centre and began a spirited dance with spears and masks. One carried a rifle that he fired enthusiastically into the air. Despite struggling with low spirits, I attempted to show some interest.

The men gave way and next came some young girls performing with the picturesque addition of garlands and baskets. Kanawha explained that the dance told the story of how the clan first learned to grow corn.

'Do all your dances tell stories?' I asked, intrigued.

Kanawha was tapping her feet in time to the drums. 'Yes, don't yours?'

'Sometimes. In the ballet, yes, I suppose they do, but not usually. Sometimes we just dance for the fun of it, men and women together.'

'Together!' She looked shocked at the suggestion. 'You teach each other the dances?'

'Of course. Rich people have dancing instructors, us poor pick it up as we go along.'

'But do men and women not have secret knowledge, dances that are passed down from father to son, mother to daughter?'

I laughed at the idea. 'No, there's nothing mysterious about our dancing. Balls – or dances – are usually about courtship – finding a mate –not about secrets.' My cheeks flushed as I remembered my own humiliation in Bath, an evening that seemed to belong to another age but in truth was less than half a year ago.

'Ah.' She nodded her head in understanding. 'Courtship, yes, I see.' Her eyes lingered on a tall man a little older than the others dancing now.

'Is that your future husband?'

'Yes.'

I watched him dance for a minute or two; he

went about it with an intensity lacking in the other performers, face set in a frown. He did not seem a very suitable match for the gay-spirited Kanawha, but then, what did I know?

There was a sudden outburst of whistling and clapping. Kanawha gripped my arm in excitement.

'Look, Tecumseh is dancing.'

My new brother had sprung to his feet and whirled into the centre of the dance. He ducked and dived, twisted and turned, performing handsprings with an agility I'd not seen since Pedro played Ariel. Obviously a favoured performer, the audience beat their appreciation with their feet. If this had been Drury Lane, they would have called for an encore. I joined in the applause at the end, jumping up in my enthusiasm.

Face shining with recent exertion, Tecumseh caught sight of me and grabbed my wrist.

'Come, sister. Kanawha say you dance for us.'

I pulled away. The idea of performing a ballet after his wild display was as incongruous as entering a boxing ring and trying to entertain the spectators with an embroidery class. 'That's not a good idea,' I begged off.

But Tecumseh was adamant, as was Kanawha, who pushed as he pulled me into the centre. The cheering died away and everyone waited expectantly.

Rescue me, I pleaded to the heavens, hoping for a friendly downpour or bolt of lightning.

Nothing.

My dithering became embarrassing. I had to do something, but dancing with no music was out of the question. I decided I would sing instead, the choice of a lesser evil. One of the wild Scottish poems by the bard Ossian came to mind. I had first heard it at a concert in the drawing room at Boxton, but the ballad seemed fitting for this company with its story of warriors and spears, wind, rain and stars. The mournful tune lifted me from that wilderness for a time, connecting me to my old life. My existence here among the Creeks had become like Thomas the Rhymer's time in faerie land: my past had faded, becoming like a dream as the new life took hold. What was Frank or Pedro to these people? Syd and Bow Street?

Drury Lane? They were myths from my history.

'My life flies away like a dream:
Why should I stay behind?'

My voice caught on these words and I could not continue.

Unaware the song had not yet finished, the Indians gave my performance a hearty round of applause. Though few had followed the words, the sad tune had appealed to these people all too familiar with loss and separation. Kanawha, however, gave me a strange look as I returned to my seat. Perhaps she alone had understood.

SCENE 3 – WHITE MEN

Weeks passed. Maclean had long since disappeared to the nearest trading post, hopefully for good, and I was getting used to my new identity as clan maiden until I had worked out what I was going to do.

Then one April morning, a canoe arrived at the landing stage carrying two white men. Those of us in the village went down to see what brought them to us. According to Kanawha, they had to be either traders or missionaries because no one else would bother to make the arduous journey to Chickamauga. I peeped out from behind Tecumseh as the men warily came ashore. The older of the two, a man with grey hair and a round brimmed hat, bowed low; his companion perched on a barrel behind him, sketching the people as they clustered around the canoe.

'I come in peace!' said Grey Hair dramatically,

holding up his hand, palm open. 'Do you understand?'

Grandmother Bee darted forward and prodded the man's big belly. She squawked with laughter. Looking discomfited, the man spoke louder, obviously thinking this would help us learn English.

'I COME IN . . .'

'We heard you first time,' said Tecumseh softly.

'Oh!' The man flushed and tried to wipe his sweating brow, but in the interim some enterprising child had made off with his silk handkerchief. 'Well, as you speak English, let me introduce myself. I am John Davies. I have come on the behest of Mr Jefferson himself and am making a tour of the district, learning about local Indian customs.'

'Come to spy out our land and steal our hunting grounds more like,' muttered Kanawha for my benefit.

I sympathized with her but that was not the reason my heart was beating so fast; to me, these men represented a lifeline. If they came from Mr

Jefferson, the American politician I had heard Johnny praise, then they were my way out of here, back to cities, ports and ships headed home to my friends.

'Please take me to your leader,' Davies continued. 'We have heard the great name of McGillivray of the Creeks and wish to pay him our respects.'

Tecumseh nodded and beckoned them to follow. Davies' eyes fell on me briefly as they set off, attention caught by my telltale red hair and pale skin. He frowned but said nothing.

I made to follow them, thinking I might be able to make my appeal for assistance, but Kanawha pulled me back.

'Leave them,' she whispered as if she knew my intention. 'They are bloodsuckers, those men, like Mac Clan.'

She was right: I should be more suspicious of my fellow whites. For all I knew, they might even be here on Maclean's behalf and I was stupidly about to cast myself on their mercy. Besides, I knew my adopted family would have a thing or two to say about my desire to leave. Only Kanawha seemed to understand my desire to escape a future others had decided for me. I had to be cleverer than that.

Tecumseh and Little Turtle came back from the meeting at the chief's house with news of the outside world – news that concerned me closely. Davies and his artist companion, one Gilbert Stuart, had told the Creeks that the American navy had chased the *Courageous* out of her waters some weeks ago. Shots had been exchanged causing casualties on both sides, but both the British and American authorities were playing the incident down, having no desire to spark off a new war over an old grudge. The citizens of the American Republic looked on the encounter as a victory and had celebrated their enemy being sent packing for the Caribbean with his tail between his legs. I heard the news with mixed feelings: the retreat meant that Maclean could no longer hold out any hope of rejoining the ship immediately, but it also meant that my friends were too far away for me to reach them – even if the *Courageous* had survived the American bombardment.

As the sun set in a blush of pink clouds, I retreated to the fence behind the house to consider the news. I refused to believe that any of my friends featured on the casualty list. Surely Syd would have kept them safe for me? With a groan, I hugged my sides for comfort, knowing I was fooling myself by assuming that Syd stood between me and the unpleasant reality of life, as he always had when we were little. He could not save Pedro from every flying splinter, or ensure that Frank manned a gun far from any hit. He himself would have been exposed as any of them to the dangers of battle. I had to face the fact that any of them could be dead.

There was a light touch on my neck, making me almost jump out of my skin. I slipped from the fence and turned to find Little Turtle standing right behind me. He leaned against the log stretched between us and patted my arm.

'You are troubled, wife.'

'Yes, I am worried for my friends,' I replied, deciding to let the wife bit pass. I'd tackle that another night when I was feeling stronger.

Little Turtle pulled me towards him and enfolded me in a reassuring hug. At first tense, I then relaxed against his chest, hearing his heart beat slow and steady. Calm seeped into me. It felt very chaste with the fence between us and I hungered for some human sympathy, having spent so long struggling to survive on my own.

'You must not worry for them,' he said. 'In your story, the bull, raven and hare were strong and clever creatures. They will find their way home.'

It was strange to be so close to a man like this. Little Turtle's voice rumbled deep in his ribs, tickling my cheek with the vibration.

Stop it, Cat. Concentrate, snapped that determined side to my character. Do not succumb to the temptation to be looked after. You have to resist if you want to be yourself and not end up as some Indian wife, one among many in Little Turtle's cabin.

I pulled myself away and gave what I hoped he would understand to be a cool smile.

'Thank you for your concern, sir.' What was I doing, addressing him as if we were in a London drawing room? 'I feel happier now.' I retreated quickly into the house before he could say another word.

Little Turtle sat next to me at supper that night, first placing in my lap a flower.

'For you,' he said with a blush. Kanawha and Tecumseh looked on approvingly, evidently pleased by their brother's newfound boldness.

I didn't have the heart to crush him so publicly, particularly after his kindness. 'Thank you,' I replied, tucking the flower into my braid. How could I tell him that I had not the least inclination to marry him? He was sweet, but the only reason my pulse beat faster when he approached was because I was fighting the desire to run for the hills.

Grandmother Bee cackled, then put her arms around us both and hugged us close. I had a sudden panic that maybe in this culture accepting a flower was tantamount to accepting his proposal. The old lady jabbered away in Creek to the other three, punctuating her talk with vigorous hand gestures, flicking my hair and pulling Little Turtle's nose. I guessed she was saying that it was about time the pair of us named the day.

I had to do something – and fast.

'Did I ever tell you, Kanawha,' I began conversationally as I stirred my bowl of stew, 'that I am betrothed to a man in England?'

The four of them stopped talking abruptly.

'Oh yes, I am pledged to him by most solemn vows, taken in the presence of my . . . my ancestors – you know, the sort of vows that are unbreakable.' A petal fell from the flower and fluttered into my lap.

Little Turtle choked on his last mouthful.

'No, Cat, you had not said. Who is this man?' Kanawha was suspicious.

'His name . . . his name . . . yes, he has a name . . .' But who? 'His name is Syd Fletcher. He is the chief warrior of my clan back in London. Thunder Fists, they call him,' (they didn't but I was getting carried away). 'He is the size of a bear and . . . and roars like a buffalo.'

Little Turtle squared his shoulders and said something in Creek to Tecumseh.

'My brother will fight him for you if he comes

here,' Tecumseh translated solemnly.

That wasn't quite what I intended. 'No, no, it is the vow that binds us, sacred to my people.' I crossed my fingers, hoping the Almighty was not listening to my lies.

But Grandmother Bee was having none of this. She poked me in the ribs and unleashed a torrent of words which Kanawha translated.

'She say that your adoption gives you new ancestors. You must make peace with the old and bring an offering to the new so that you can start your life as a Creek. No word binds you. It is as if you died.'

'That's not how I feel about –'

'It does not matter what you feel,' Tecumseh interrupted. 'You are Creek daughter now. You will go into forest and fast for four days. Then you will offer gifts to the old ancestors and to the new. In that time, your spirit guide will reveal itself to you and make peace between them.'

'My what?'

'Your animal guardian.'

My reason revolted against the idea; I had been

brought up in a world that didn't believe in such primitive superstitions.

'I'm sorry but I don't think so –'

Grandmother Bee clipped me round the ear, sending the flower flying. I jumped indignantly to my feet; I had had enough of being pushed around.

'I just said that I didn't want to do it!' I exclaimed. 'What's wrong with being honest?'

Grandmother shook her fist and continued to scold me.

The feelings that had been brewing in me now boiled over. 'Look, you all know I don't fit in here – I'm a fish out of water – a . . . a cuckoo in the nest – I don't know what words you people use to say it but I just want to go home – *my home*, not yours!'

Little Turtle looked up at me reproachfully. Grandmother Bee dragged on my hand, placing it in his, snapping away at me in a stream of reproofs. I snatched my hand back.

'I don't want to marry! Why can't you just leave me alone?' I snarled.

The old lady turned her attention to her oldest

grandson, urging him in her voluble manner to do something about this rebellion under her roof. Using the same calm approach he did with the horses, Tecumseh waited for her to finish, then spoke gently to me.

'Sit down, Girl Cat.'

I was still on my feet, fuming. I had worked myself up into such a passion, there seemed no graceful way of stepping back from it. I had also managed to insult Little Turtle in front of his family.

'Sit down,' Tecumseh repeated, this time with a hint of firmness.

'I prefer to stand.' I crossed my arms on my chest.

'I asked you to sit.'

Kanawha edged to my side and tugged at my tunic. I resisted, unsure what to do. I had never been part of a family before and knew nothing of a brother's discipline.

Tecumseh rose and moved to stand in front of me, meeting my gaze. 'Sit.' He pressed my shoulders down. There seemed little choice but to do as ordered or turn this into an unseemly scuffle.

Tecumseh addressed the others, his eyes mainly on Little Turtle: 'When our chief gave Girl Cat into our care, I knew that we would have many troubles with her. She is Sasakwa: the horse that shies from the bridle.'

My 'family' murmured their agreement. Little Turtle gave a rueful smile. I continued to seethe.

'I say that she shall do as Grandmother says,' announced Tecumseh. 'If this vow exists, she must ask humbly to be released from it. Then she must find out which animal has taken on the burden of being her guide before she marries our brother.'

'But I don't –'

Tecumseh held up a finger to silence me. 'She has to learn to accept the bridle; she can no longer run free on the savannah. She must take her place among us.'

The pressure on me was enormous. I could now understand how Kanawha had been brought to accept a man she did not like; it wasn't through beatings and threats but having to bear the weight of the expectations of others, of your nearest and dearest. But I was not broken in yet – and never would be. I was Cat Royal of Drury Lane still. They compared me to that devilish horse? Well then, that's how I would act: submit to what I had to, resist when I could. Sasakwa's spirit was not yet cowed either.

'I will seek the animal guide you speak of,' I said, 'but do not be surprised when none claims me. Perhaps then you will believe me when I say I do not belong here.'

'And the vow?' Tecumseh asked.

'There was no vow. I . . . er . . . lied.'

He smiled. I guessed he had known or suspected that all along. 'So why not tell your family the truth?'

'Because I did not want to offend Little Turtle.' My designated husband-to-be looked almost disappointed that there was no Thunder Fists to defeat. 'I was trying to tell you that I do not want to marry anyone.'

'Then you must ask the ancestors forgiveness for your crooked words. Your fast begins tomorrow at dawn,' Tecumseh declared, filling my bowl with a second helping of stew.

Grandmother woke me before sunrise and led me out into the forest. She allowed me to take nothing but the clothes I stood up in and a knife, whether to defend myself or to cut the fruit for the ancestors, I don't know. It was scant protection against larger predators; I just hoped she knew what she was doing.

We walked all morning until the trees began to thin and we came out on the crest of a hill overlooking a grassy plain. There was barely a tree or bush to be seen: it appeared as a kind of vast bowl surrounded by forested hills, open to the heavens. Grandmother patted the ground beneath a giant magnolia tree. It was an impressive sight, covered with lush pinkish-white flowers and decorated with wooden chimes, strips of cloth and beads; it was evidently a special place for the Wind Clan.

'The savannah,' she said in her broken English, indicating the plain with a sweep of her arm. 'Place where Girl Cat run no longer. Forest – ' she pointed behind her, 'now your home. Sit here and think.'

'How long do I have to wait?' I asked, already having had my fill of the wilderness.

'Four days.' She passed me a waterskin. 'Drink only. I come for you. Do not get lost.'

With that, the old lady disappeared back into the forest.

With four days ahead of me, I had better make myself comfortable. I crossed my legs and gazed upon the scene before me. As soon as my body stopped humming with energy, resting from the strenuous walk, my mind began to whirl with thoughts. What was I doing here, Reader, so far from my natural element, the streets of London? It seemed incredible that I had got myself in this fix, yet I knew I was not the first. I'd heard travellers' tales of people adopted by Indian tribes and stories of Indian princesses coming to London; it was not really so impossible – except for the fact that it was happening to me.

An hour passed. By now the birds and beasts had become used to my presence under the tree. One by one they re-emerged. First a turkey cock ventured out from the trees to peck at my feet, its comb wobbling like a high curled fop's wig. A herd of deer poured from the trees and scattered on to the plain to graze, bringing with them the poignant recollection of my ride with Frank when we had watched the deer run across his estate. A flock of large white birds – cranes, I think they were – flew overhead, legs dangling behind. They landed not far away on a fallen tree, calling to each other in their urgent voices, like an excited audience in the galleries for a first night. Shadows moved across the grass in the distance – horses or maybe even buffalo – it was hard to tell from this distance. Insects hummed and butterflies flitted from flower to flower; everything was busy, everything was at home – except me.

By late afternoon, I was feeling bad-tempered and hungry. I have never aspired to be a hermit and if this enforced retreat was supposed to be a spiritual experience, then it was passing me by. As for animal guides, the only thing that had come near me all day was the turkey; under no circumstances was Cat Royal going to have a turkey as her life's guardian.

I slept little that night, getting up frequently to try and warm myself by pacing to and fro. I had no materials to start a fire and none of the woodcraft needed to do it from scratch. I was beginning to fantasize about hot baths and lavish dinners. I talked aloud to myself, sang – anything to keep from despair.

Day two. I hate turkeys. I refuse to be adopted by one.

Day three. When you have nothing to eat for so long, your stomach seems to contract so that it forms a fist, punching away inside you: 'Remember me?' it says, 'Fill me!'

I told it to shut up. I was determined to honour the expectations of my Creek hosts even if I didn't believe in the virtues of fasting. Besides, if I could survive the ship's hold, I could survive this!

The stars were particularly fine that night, huge sweeps of spangles sprinkled across the velvet heavens like the most expensive fabric in a dressmaker's window. With a melancholy feeling of homesickness, I recalled how Frank had told me that the stars were each suns far, far away, but I could not imagine that. Pedro had once said they told stories – now that I could believe. According to legend, Greek heroes often ended up there when they died; I wondered if the Creeks thought that was where their great warriors went? The home of the ancestors with whom I was supposed to be making my peace? Well, the stars looked pretty peaceful to me, not bothered by my falsehoods or my little fretful life. They had better things to do.

Lying under the magnolia, I began to wonder about my own ancestors – a short speculation as I have no idea who my parents were. But if they had died after I was born, did that mean they would be watching me now from somewhere up there? Were they wondering why their daughter was under a tree ignoring the attentions of a friendly turkey?

The snap of a twig brought me to my senses. Something was approaching through the bushes behind me. Over the past few days, I had tried not to think too much about possible predators, but bears had never been absent from my imagination.

It would be just my luck to find my spirit guardian wanted to eat me. I grasped the hilt of my knife and strained my ears. The creature blundered nearer, stumbled and swore – in English. My blood ran cold.

Like a shot, I scrambled up the tree but a fist gripped my ankle and pulled me to the ground. Maclean – I had known the moment I had heard him swear.

'There was a rumour you were turning Creek, you little savage,' he said triumphantly, kneeling on my back as he roped my hands. 'Undergoing the rites of passage, the Yankee said, under the tribe's big magnolia tree. He said he's going to dedicate a whole chapter to you when he writes up his notes.' My ankles were now knotted viciously together. 'Wants to talk to you for your unique cultural insights, but he's not going to get a chance, is he? Shame, you could've been the toast of Philadelphia's drawing rooms.'

I turned my head away. I felt too weak from fasting even to curse – my spirits too depressed. All the fight seemed to have gone out of me. 'Why did you come back?' I asked. 'You must know the *Courageous* has sailed. I can be of no use to you now.'

Maclean plumped himself down in my spot and took out a tinder box. He lit a fire and made himself comfortable, filled a pipe and, between puffs, chewed on some salted pork from his pack.

'Look at it another way,' he said at last. 'You're all I've got now. I had the money for taking you out of the country, but, thanks to you, I won't get nothing for seeing the job through to the end. I should've dumped you all in the Bristol Channel, not tried to follow the orders of my squeamish paymaster.'

'So what are you going to do with me?' I wriggled into a sitting position. He hadn't killed or beaten me as I had expected – he must have some other plan in mind.

'I'm going to ransom you.' He brushed some crumbs to the floor. My stomach clenched but I knew better than to expect anything from him.

'Ransom me? What do you mean?'

He lay at his ease, head propped on his

bundle. 'That's my reserve plan. I always had it in mind in case things went wrong, otherwise I would never have risked bringing you on to the *Courageous*. That young lord cares for you – that's plain to see – so I'm planning to buy myself a new life, thanks to you.'

'You're taking me to Frank?' Despite being disgusted that I was to be bartered like a cow at market, I felt a glimmer of hope. 'Do you know where he is then?'

'Nope.' Maclean started on a loaf of bread. 'My guess is that he's in the West Indies.' He let the silence regroup around us as he chewed his mouthful, tantalizing me with crumbs of news. Hacking off another slice, he continued, 'And for news to get back to his parents – well, let's say it could be several months before he's in funds. That's unless he has the good fortune to fall in with someone he knows in Jamaica.'

That was very possible; some of Frank's schoolfellows came from the Indies. While not his friends, they could at least vouch for him.

'My bet is that he won't return to England by

himself; he'll be out looking for you.' He prodded me with his foot and laughed. 'And if I were him, I'd start where I last saw you. That's why I'm taking you back to the fort. Just think about that: you've come all this way for nothing.'

The thought seemed to please him mightily.

At that moment, my turkey ill-advisedly wandered out of the trees to pay me his accustomed visit. He did not realize that the situation had dramatically changed. Seeing his friendly strut in our direction, Maclean went still and waited for him to peck within reach – then leapt upon him and wrung his neck before the poor bird knew what had hit him. My captor threw the carcass down in front of me and sat me up to release my hands.

'My lucky night, eh?' He prodded the still warm bird with his foot. 'About time you earned your keep – pluck it for my breakfast. And don't even think of trying to escape!'

It felt the worst kind of violation of my four-day fast to rip out the feathers of the creature that was my closest thing to a spirit guardian. With my back to Maclean, I fought the temptation to give way to furious sobs as I prepared the carcass. It seemed so like a white man not even to think before taking for himself, having no interest or respect for the sacred place we were in. And what was I to do now? I was only one step better off than the turkey, trussed up here at Maclean's mercy. I couldn't stomach the thought of allowing him to drag me about for months, a passive hostage he could use to reward his own vicious behaviour. He'd soon fall to beating me again, I had no doubt. I felt sick with rage at my powerlessness.

I pulled out the poor creature's tail and slipped a stubby quill into my pocket as a keepsake, begging his forgiveness as I did so. It made me think of the fine goose feather pens I had enjoyed in Boxton. Why, I wondered, had I done so little writing when I had the chance, instead wasting my time fretting with boredom? It was too late now: the pen was out of my hand. On all sides I was beset with people who were trying to write my tale. But I wanted to be me again: not Creek wife, not bargaining chip, but Cat.

As the feathers of my dead guardian fluttered in the air, the answer came to me. I had nothing to lose, that was my one advantage. If I stayed with the Creeks or Maclean, I might as well be dead. I was ready to risk everything to live as me.

Maclean knew that the Creeks were coming back for me on the fourth day so he made us set off early. As we walked in file, my hands bound behind me once more, he chewed a turkey drumstick. Despite my hunger, I refused to touch the meat. My suffering put him in a good humour, making him more garrulous than usual. He told me he had left Chickamauga only to purchase a canoe at the trading post, always intending to come back for me. It had never entered his mind to respect the chief's pronouncement that I now belonged to the tribe.

He had moored his boat downstream of the village, which meant we were to skirt round Chickamauga and strike the river several miles from the landing stage, so avoiding all Creeks.

'I suppose you should be thanking me, girl,' he

commented, throwing the bone into the bushes. 'I saved you from these savages. I can't see you relishing life with a husband who has a row of scalps nailed to the hut door and a bunch of little brown babies.' He chuckled at the picture. My anger flared, this time directed mainly at myself, for part of me was grateful to escape marriage to Little Turtle. But to hear it in his words made me wonder: was I too proud, too prejudiced to accept an honourable man of a different race? They weren't my reasons surely? Maclean was still speaking.

'If your lordling stands by you, there's no reason why you can't see civilization again.'

But I had my doubts my captor would let me live to be a witness to his treachery. Unless Frank was very careful, Maclean would cheat him: he would kill me and have another stab at Frank if given the chance.

'The moment I see civilization will come as soon as I see the back of you,' I retorted.

He laughed at me. 'Fancy yourself as a wit, do you, girl? Well, it seems to me you're at least half a one.'

'Very funny.'

The trees were getting denser, festooned with the bearded growths that I remembered from the swamp. Maclean cut through them with a stout wooden-handled blade. 'You know, I never understood how a girl brought up in the theatre could fall for it. I thought you'd smoke us out for sure, but he was right. You were all fooled.'

'What are you talking about?'

'Work it out – it doesn't matter now if you do. I don't care if he gets the blame as long as I'm paid for your ransom. In fact, I'd rather like him to be found out for all the trouble he's given me.'

'Blame? Blame for what?'

Maclean gave a tug on my rope to signal a stop. 'I tell you what: you guess who betrayed you and I'll give you something to eat.' He unwrapped his picnic and settled down to ease his legs.

Hands still bound, I sat with my head on my knees, faint with hunger. Black blots swam before my eyes. I knew what he was saying was important but I couldn't think, not like this. He must be talking about Frank's enemy, but why would my theatre upbringing make me less likely to fall for their plot? Was he talking about some actor, someone assuming a character that wasn't theirs? No, that didn't make sense. He had to mean something else.

I closed my eyes, thinking back to the time I spent in Bath. With every day that passed, the idea that Billy Shepherd had been behind the plot had seemed less and less likely. He certainly was no squeamish paymaster. If he wanted Frank out of the way, he would have had him killed in that alley, not risked sending him away. He would not be so faint-hearted – he might even do the deed himself. Then it suddenly came to me that Billy had always said he wanted the privilege of killing me himself, so he would not have handed me over to Maclean, surely? Too late for it to be of any use, I realized that it was safe to rule out Billy Shepherd.

Who did that leave on my list of suspects? Unspecified jealous suitors? This seemed so very unlikely. The unknown second cousin and Mr Dixon? One I'd never met and the other had been gravely injured. The moment of my nightmares flashed through my mind again – the bloodied hands, the screaming, the blow.

Wait a moment! I went rigid as it suddenly all made sense. The men who had run towards us had been armed with clubs; I'd not seen a blade anywhere. How could Dixon have sustained a belly cut when none of the rest of us had been threatened by a knife?

I was so, so stupid. I bashed my forehead on my knees, thumping myself for my blockheadedness. Of course I knew how he'd done it. I'd lived behind the scenes, hadn't I? I'd even helped strap on the blood pack, as we called it, to give the added touch of realism to the fatal ends of most tragedies – blood from Syd's butcher's shop, contained in a pouch and punctured by the actor or a well-judged thrust of a stage sword at the appropriate moment. Not popular with the laundresses but a favourite with the crowd.

Dixon had tricked us! He had lured us into the trap so that he could get his hands on Frank's fortune. Having staged our abduction, he 'survived' to give the worst construction of my part in the business. No wonder the magistrate had been after me so quickly! Who would doubt such an eyewitness? Not even the duke and duchess would think to question Dixon's sworn statement that they had harboured a viper at the heart of their family. Indeed, they had given home to one, but it had not been me.

And I had thought Dixon a gentleman. I'd even liked him for his gallant attentions. It was disconcerting to realize that he had obviously had the lowest of low opinions about me from the start if he thought throwing me on board a ship suitable punishment for my pretensions. But that was nothing set against Frank's love for his cousin: that was a betrayal of the worst kind.

'Dixon.' I said the word softly.

A hunk of bread was thrown into my lap and my hands untied.

I had guessed rightly.

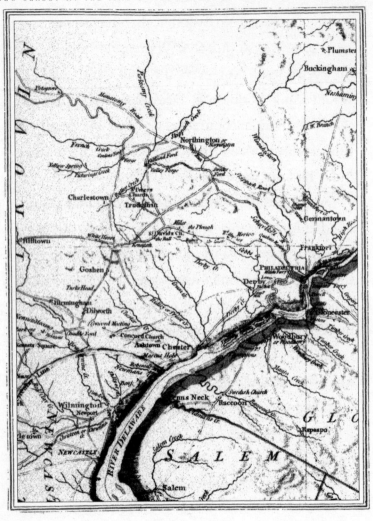

Act V — In which Cat takes
a gamble ...

Act V

SCENE 1 – LIFE OR DEATH?

The revelation as to who had caused our suffering revived my flagging spirits. I was determined now to risk everything to get free of Maclean and do my best to see justice done. A knot of hatred towards my captor formed in my chest, hard and fierce, stronger and more bitter than anything I had ever felt. I watched him as he strode so confidently ahead of me, pulling me along like a tethered calf. Always someone's agent: first for Captain Barton on his murderous raid, now Dixon and his greedy ambition – it was about time the purser got his comeuppance. I prayed that God would see fit to use me as His agent in making that come to pass.

By my calculations I had two advantages: one was a desperate desire to escape, and the second, something Maclean had completely under-estimated: the Creeks. I knew that they would come after me once they discovered me gone from the magnolia tree.

Late afternoon. Shafts of sunlight pierced the tree canopy obliquely, spotlighting a stream tumbling down the wooded hillside. The water sparkled and frothed, crashing from rock to rock, drowning out all other sounds. Incredibly to my eyes, brown fish flashed into the air as they leapt against the tide, struggling up the fall. Maclean gazed on the sight, greatly pleased.

'Not far now,' he said. 'This is the stream I followed when I hid the boat and came in search of you.' He checked our position on a map someone had sketched for him – that wretched artist, I guessed. It showed the magnolia tree, Chicka-mauga and the river.

I said nothing, watching a fish flail against the odds up to a higher ledge. Its tenacity was awe-inspiring, chiming with something inside me.

'Picturesque, isn't it?' he commented ironically, waving his hand towards the lip of a particularly long fall. 'That's what your fine folks would say if they were here. But no need for us to get our feet wet – there's a path of sorts down this side.' He gave me a shove in the back. 'You go first: I don't want you tripping and tumbling on top of me.'

'Will you untie my hands?' I asked, not liking the look of the rocky path he expected me to climb down.

'No. You take your chance as you are. I don't want you running off now.'

I didn't bother to protest, but began to descend. The stones were wet and slippery. Inevitably, I lost my footing and slid to a broad ledge jutting out over the fall. I would have gone over had I not been jerked to a stop by the rope he still held.

'Idiot!' he bellowed, leaping down after me and hauling me to my feet. My legs and back were grazed and I had twisted my ankle. The spray from the waterfall fell around us like fine rain, soaking us both.

'I need my hands! I can't climb without my hands!' I shouted back over the noise of the thundering water.

Just then an arrow skittered to the ground at

our feet. Maclean sprang round as if he had been stung.

'Damnation! Indians!' he cursed, ungallantly pulling me in front of him as a shield.

Unheard and unseen until the very last moment, my Creek family emerged from the trees. Kanawha already had another arrow fitted to her bow. Tecumseh stepped forward.

'You take my sister without leave,' he said sternly. 'Let her go.'

Maclean felt under the skirt of his long jacket and pulled out a pistol, another purchase from the trading post that he had kept quiet about. He levelled the gun first at Tecumseh, then, thinking better of that, at my temple.

'I told you, Indian, the girl's my business. One step nearer and I'll kill her.'

Tecumseh hesitated. His eyes flicked from me to the fall behind us.

'We cannot let you take her. She is family. That is our law.'

I braced myself, planting my feet firmly on the ground. If only that pistol was not at my temple, I would put my rash plan into action; but move now and I'd be dead before I had a chance.

Maclean felt me shift and pressed the barrel even closer into my flesh. 'But just at the moment, it's my law that matters and I say I take her or I take her life – an easy choice, Indian. Do you prefer the girl alive or dead?'

Kanawha had her lips pressed close together, trying to get a clear shot at Maclean.

'Tell your Amazon to put down her bow,' continued Maclean. 'You must retreat.'

Tecumseh met my eyes; I think he intuitively understood my thoughts. I wanted no one to die; there would be other opportunities. He nodded and put a hand on Kanawha's shoulder. She lowered the arrow.

'Ayaah!' With a war cry of pure fury, a third Indian leapt from the other side of the stream across the waterfall, landing on the ledge behind us. Maclean spun me round in surprise and discharged the pistol at our attacker. Little Turtle clutched his chest and tumbled down from the rock, landing on the shelf below. I screamed in shock and fury. I didn't want this for me – not bloodshed.

'Very stupid!' Maclean shouted, throwing the now empty pistol aside and dragging the wooden-handled blade out of his belt. He held it out in front of us. 'Attack again and *she* dies.'

Tecumseh made to go to the rescue of his brother, who was groaning on the rock below.

'Don't move!' warned Maclean, shuffling backwards.

That was my chance. I used the backwards momentum and pushed hard, catching him unawares. His arm still across my chest, we tumbled over the edge into the waterfall. I can remember the sensation of freefall – the brief, terrifying exhilaration of letting go of life with no hope or expectation of surviving. My hands were bound – I couldn't swim, but at last I had had it in my power to make a choice and I'd chosen to be free.

Perhaps the fact that I am able to write this has told you that my tale has not quite come to its end. I owe you, Reader, an account of what happened next even though it pains me to do so.

We hit the water with stunning force. Maclean let go of me, intent on his own survival. I sank, pulled down in the boiling currents of the pool. All was confusion. My lungs burned, crying out for me to breathe. Things brushed past me: rocks, fish, debris. I could see nothing, knew nothing.

Then one touch firmed into a grip. I was hauled upwards and broke the surface to take a gasp of wonderful air. Another hand seized the back of my shirt and hauled me to the side. I lay there, coughing water; it was enough to feel rock under my cheek.

'Cat!' Kanawha slapped my back, dripping water over me as she leant forward and cut my ropes. I guessed I now knew who had leapt into the pool to save me.

'I'm all right. Little Turtle?'

She did not reply, but ran back up the rocky path at the side of the waterfall. Having helped haul me on shore, Tecumseh had already rushed to his brother's aid. I could see the two Indians cradling Little Turtle, Tecumseh rocking to and fro in grief, his clothes stained with blood. Kanawha let out a cry that echoed through the forest, louder even than the roar of the waterfall.

Struck in the heart by Maclean's bullet, Little Turtle had bled swiftly to death. A red stream trickled from his body and dripped over the edge of the fall to the water.

The Creeks found Maclean as he attempted to escape downriver in his boat. He was brought back that night to Chickamauga and locked in a granary as his case was not to be heard until the clan had paid tribute to the fallen warrior. I watched from the edge of the circle of torches as everyone else from the village gathered around the totem in the centre, grieving loudly for a man who had been well liked for his shyness, modesty and loyalty. Kanawha was inconsolable. Grandmother Bee's face was set, betraying only fierce anger as yet another of her kin was claimed by death. Tecumseh led the ceremony with rigid dignity, though I could see he was holding back a storm of emotions.

As for me, I was numb. I had been prepared to risk my own life, but I had never meant to be the cause of someone else's death. I knew that no one blamed me – their anger was saved for Maclean – but I blamed myself.

My eye was caught by the two Americans, standing like me at the edge of the circle. Davies was taking notes, Stuart was sketching the litter on which they had placed Little Turtle. I marched over and ripped the pad out of the artist's hands before he knew what had hit him.

'Have you no respect?' I hissed at him, tearing the drawing into confetti.

Davies tucked his notebook in his pocket before that too shared the same fate.

Stuart shrugged. 'It's only an Indian.'

Whack! I slapped him hard around the face. Stuart was too astounded to react.

'He may be only an Indian to you, but to me, he was a friend, a brother.' I turned to glare at Davies, who was eyeing me with interest. 'And don't you dare put that in your book, you, you vulture!'

'And how do you propose to stop me, young woman?' he asked arrogantly. He seemed amused rather than angry at my intervention. 'Do you not know that the conquerors always write the history books?'

'Conquerors?' I spat. 'All I see is a white man who thinks he knows it all.'

'You are English, aren't you?' Davies noted.

'So?'

'Well, you might like to reflect that it was your nation among others that brought this civilization down. I am merely riding in the wagons behind that conquering army. You are looking at the last of a great race.' He nodded at Tecumseh, Killbuck and the other men who had now shouldered the litter to take Little Turtle into the forest. I bowed my head as they passed.

'You see, my dear,' Davies continued, 'there is no changing the outcome. America belongs to the white man now. You can do nothing to alter that.'

'Perhaps not. But there is something I can do,' I muttered as the men disappeared into the trees.

Davies gave me a patronizing smile. 'But what can a girl do against the forces of history?'

'You're not the only one who can write.' I turned on my heel and left the circle of torches.

Maclean's trial took place the following morning. The men of the village sat in a circle; Maclean was forced to kneel in the centre, his arms bound. He looked ashen: he knew that the Indians had it in their power to execute him and doubtless he was imagining all sorts of horrible ends. I have never shared my fellow Londoners' love of a good hanging, but for once I could understand what drove us to take a life in revenge. It was a cold kind of satisfaction that did nothing to heal the grief, but it was all the living could offer the spirits of the dead.

No sooner had I thought this than the conviction formed in my breast that Little Turtle would not want to be honoured in this way. He had loved music, dancing, jokes, his family; an execution would have saddened him.

Most of those gathered, however, were after

Maclean's blood. The charges were listed against him: murder, abduction, violation of a sacred place. Seeing him cowering before Chief McGillivray, I wondered what had driven Maclean to be as he was? His cruelty had been so implacable from the beginning, yet he also showed signs of being an educated man; how could he have become the savage that knelt before all these good people? I remembered that Mrs Foster had told me that he had once been in training to be a priest but had been forced to sea by poverty. Had this soured him, turned him from his beliefs in a loving and compassionate God? Or maybe he had never truly believed what he was to preach?

Trying to put myself in the shoes of my enemy was making my head spin and complicating my feelings. It was easier to hate, much harder to understand.

The chief raised his hands and the talk died away. He pronounced his judgement in English for the benefit of the prisoner.

'Mac Clan is guilty of murder. The penalty I leave to the family to decide.' He turned to

Tecumseh and handed him an axe. 'It is your right to take his life. Or you can demand compensation.'

Maclean bent his head, expecting the blow to fall. At least he was taking his sentence with dignity, something I had not expected.

With a whooping cry, Tecumseh brandished the axe – and threw it into the earth in front of Maclean.

'My brother is gone and no death can bring him back. But his loss must be honoured: I ask that Maclean serve our clan for the rest of his worthless life.'

McGillivray nodded. 'Your words are wise, my brother. A white man's death would bring vengeance on us no matter what his crime. He will be taken to the clan grounds on Smoke Ridge and will work for us there.' He turned to the purser. 'Do not think to escape. It is far from any village and we will hunt you down if you run.'

I remembered Tecumseh's words as to the three alternatives facing captives: death, adoption or slavery. Maclean was about to taste the bitter fate of the slave; it was no more than he deserved.

The trial over, Maclean was led away. As he passed me, he spat at my feet, but he had no power over me now and such gestures were futile. I did not doubt he was still hoping for some last-minute reprieve but I could not see where help would come from. He could hardly appeal to Davies and Stuart; his part in the American wars had made him no friend of theirs. If they found out who he really was, he would be facing jail in white man's territory as well as here. He would have to be content to be a footnote in Davies' book on the administration of Indian justice.

Serves him right.

'Approach, Girl Cat.'

My thoughts were broken into by McGillivray's voice. My heart skipped a beat. What had I done wrong? I had broken my fast unwillingly but maybe the violation had to be punished?

'Do not fear,' the chief said, seeing the panic on my face. 'We have to discuss your future.'

I stumbled into the centre of the circle and sat down at Tecumseh's side.

'We have some things to say together, Girl Cat, and some decisions to take.'

I nodded. After the fall into the water, I had given little thought to tomorrow. I still wanted to get away but the possibility was more remote than ever now that I owed Kanawha and her brothers my life. I might not be officially a slave like Maclean, but I felt I had a debt to repay.

'First, the ancestors have shown us your spirit guide. Puse Fo say that your willingness to throw yourself into the water, and the fact that you survived, means that it is the leaping trout.'

A murmur of agreement went round the circle. McGillivray bent forward and placed a leather thong round my neck. I grasped the necklace in my fist, feeling the wooden fish that hung from it. The carving fitted snugly in my palm.

'But like the fish I fear that you only come upstream for a brief time before returning to the ocean,' McGillivray continued.

What was this?

'Your intended mate is dead but no other warrior will wish to wed with the girl with witch-words, fearing you are ill luck.'

Tecumseh put his hand consolingly on my back, but I could hardly contain the explosion of relief inside me. If I understood rightly, I didn't have to marry; I didn't even have to ask to leave: they were throwing me out.

'But I would not willingly consign a maiden to a life among us without a husband, to an empty hut and no children to make her old age comfortable. So what must we do? The ancestors have spoken to me. They said that when you fell, you died again; you passed through the water and emerged to a new life. This has broken the ties that bound you to us.'

'You want me to go?' I asked hesitantly.

He turned the question round. 'Do you want to go?'

I bit my lip, thinking of the family into which I had so briefly been welcomed; of course I wanted to go, but it would not be without regrets.

'Yes, I want to swim back to my ocean, but I will leave part of me here.'

'That is as it should be. You are still Girl Cat of

the Wind Clan, even if you swim far from your spawning grounds, little fish.'

That was all very well, but unlike the trout I could not travel to the sea by my own fins. 'How am I to go?'

McGillivray smiled. 'I have spoken to Mr Davies. After some persuasion, he said that he would escort you to Philadelphia, but only if you promise to behave.' He took a puff of his long-stemmed pipe. 'It was noticed that Mr Stuart had a bruised cheek this morning.'

A chuckle fluttered around the group.

'I'll try to behave,' I promised.

'Then, farewell, my sister. Like the fish, may your spirit find its way home when your time comes to join our ancestors.'

My parting from my family was a more private affair, but a painful one. Grandmother Bee gripped my wrist tightly as she gabbled advice to me, advice I could not follow, but I understood that she had taken me into her heart and wished for my happiness. Leaving the clan seemed an undeserved punishment to her – a fate worse than death – and I had a hard time persuading her that I held no grudge for my banishment. She pressed upon me a bundle of medicines, rapidly explaining their uses, evidently determined that I should have a cure for most of life's ills. Once my pack was full, she then patted my chest.

'No cure for broken heart,' she muttered in English, wiping away a tear.

I knew that she was thinking of Little Turtle and so I kissed her on the brow.

'No, nothing can mend that,' I agreed.

Kanawha gave me her spare bow and a set of arrows.

'So you do not go hungry,' she explained, her eyes bright with unshed tears.

'Thank you, sister,' I replied, a lump in my throat. 'I owe you my life but I have nothing to give in return.'

'Sisters have no need of payment. You are part of me.'

I hugged her tight, wondering for the first time if I was doing the right thing by turning my back on the family I had so long sought.

Tecumseh's gift was generous beyond my expectations. The morning of my departure, he led me to the paddock and handed me Sasakwa's bridle.

'White men go back to their horses at the trading post. You will need a mount for your journey. Sasakwa is yours.' The pony snorted and bolted for the other end of the field. Tecumseh's mouth wrinkled into a smile. 'Or should I say, you are Sasakwa's. Look after her. Check her feet as I showed you. See to her comfort before yours each time you stop; then I think she will serve you well.'

He handed me a brightly coloured blanket for her back, sacks of fodder and a brush to groom her coat.

'The blanket belonged to my brother. He would have liked you to have it.'

My eyes filled with tears at the mention of Little Turtle. I felt overwhelmed by Tecumseh's kindness. 'Thank you. You have all been so good to me and I have brought you only trouble.'

He rested his hand on my shoulder. 'No, trouble followed you but you are not to blame. We do not regret that our paths crossed. You will always be our sister no matter where your fate takes you – remember that.'

SCENE 2 – PHILADELPHIA

It did not take someone with the brains of Newton to work out that the two Americans were not pleased to have me as a third in their little party, but they did not dare refuse Chief McGillivray's personal request. They had thought they were returning to Philadelphia in triumph with tales of their travels in the wilderness; now they were forced to bring a bit of the wild home with them and were not sure how it would be received. I heard Mr Davies mutter that I made a better impression in a book than in reality: more romantic and less scruffy.

Harsh – but true.

Tecumseh led me by forest trails to the trading post while the Yankees made their way by river. At our rendezvous, my brother solemnly entrusted me to Mr Davies' care.

'Look after my sister,' he said. 'Do not doubt that we will hear if any harm befalls her.'

Mr Davies bristled indignantly. 'No need to threaten me, young man. I am a gentleman.'

Tecumseh shrugged; he had met too many white 'gentlemen' to put much faith in their words.

'Don't worry about me,' I said in parting. 'I know how to handle them.'

Sasakwa butted me in the back derisively.

'This is farewell,' Tecumseh said, kissing my forehead. 'May you reach your friends in safety.'

'And you. Carry my love to our sister Kanawha and our grandmother.'

He smiled at my recognition of the family ties. 'We will think of you often.'

'And I you.' I hesitated. 'Would you do one thing for me, brother?'

He nodded.

'Would you talk to Kanawha about her feelings for her future husband? I think she is too in awe of you to admit that she does not like him.'

He began to laugh. 'Kanawha, in awe!'

'Yes.' His laughter died as he saw I was serious. Tecumseh bowed his head. 'I did not know.'

'There has been too much unhappiness in the

family. She deserves to be loved by her husband and love him in return, don't you think?'

He cupped my chin in his hand, looking deep into my eyes for a moment. 'You are wise for your years, my sister. It is true that I wish for her happiness more than anything else. I will talk to her on my return.'

'Thank you.'

He helped me on to the back of Sasakwa and slapped the pony on the rump.

'Ride well!'

I waved as the pony lurched forward. When I turned round, Tecumseh had already vanished into the trees.

Mr Stuart was putting his drawing things away. 'A fine-looking savage that,' he commented to Mr Davies.

I spurred my horse level with him. The artist held his pad to his chest defensively. I gave him a wicked grin and shifted my bow over my shoulder.

'Long way we travel together,' I commented, my voice naturally dropping into the speech pattern of an Indian.

'Yes, indeed,' he replied, licking his lips nervously.

'Many dark nights.' I adjusted the knife strapped to my waist.

'True.'

'Perhaps you like me to look after your sketch for you?'

He fumbled inside his pad and ripped out a page. 'If that will make you happy.'

'Very happy.' I folded the picture of Tecumseh and tucked it inside my jerkin. 'Thank you, sir. I am most obliged.' Back to the language of the drawing room, I gave him a wave and urged Sasakwa onwards.

Our journey to Philadelphia was long and arduous, made all the more tedious by the lack of fellowship between me and my escorts. I suppose that was partly my fault as I kept them on edge with my erratic archery practice and hours devoted to honing my knife. Neither was my dark mood reassuring as I was grieving for Little Turtle and struggling with contradictory feelings of regret that I had caused his death, and (I am ashamed to admit it) relief that I had not had to marry him and remain in the village. I didn't want to think this way but I could not hide from myself that I was thankful now I was truly heading home.

We spent two weeks riding to the coast to the nearest port and then took passage in a northward-bound sloop. Sasakwa did not like the confinement below decks, but there was no choice if she was to come with me. The pony was my only possession of value – not that she felt like mine. I could now understand how the Indians might feel they did not own anything; I regarded her as my partner in this adventure and doubted I could bring myself to sell her on arrival in white man's country, not unless I could no longer look after her myself.

My dearest hope was that I would have to do no such thing as our little ship was bound for Philadelphia. And that meant one thing: it was the home of Johnny and Lizzie. As we drew nearer, I felt my excitement growing. I knew I was lucky to have a haven on this side of the Atlantic and friends who would open their doors to me no matter what scandalous things I was said to have done. Even if they had heard the story that I'd harmed Frank, I could trust them to wait to hear my side before passing judgement. If only I could get as far as their doorstep, I could collapse, safe in the knowledge that they would take care of me and sort out the sorry muddle I was in.

But that all lay at the end of the voyage. For the moment, my presence on board the trading vessel caused much comment and speculation. I made a strange sight, dressed like a Creek and carrying nothing with me but a bow and quiver of arrows. Some sailors found it hard to believe that I was an English girl under all that Indian gear and decided to check until they were warned off in no uncertain terms – a threat involving an arrow and their manhood. I must say this for Mr Davies, he did his duty and complained about the sailors' impertinence to the captain and I was left alone for the remainder of the voyage.

Arriving in Philadelphia proved to be more of a shock than I had anticipated. I had become so used to the wilderness that the forest of masts and cliffs of warehouses around the port seemed like something from a past life. But in that jungle of civilization lay my friends' house; I only had to suffer a few more hours of this and I would be safe. I could hardly bear the delay. It was late in the afternoon when the captain unloaded us and our horses on Penn's landing. Holding tightly on to Sasakwa's bridle, I stood on the planks bewildered by the crowds of people, stevedores, sailors and beggars.

'Now, young woman, my bargain with your chief ends here,' Mr Davies announced. 'You must make your own way now.'

I nodded, too dazed to think straight. My confusion must have stirred some vestiges of decent concern in the man.

'Do you know where you are going?' he asked.

I cudgelled my brains, trying to remember Johnny and Lizzie's address. 'Yes, I have friends in Market Street.'

Davies looked relieved that he did not have to be responsible for me. 'That is easy to find: head for Christ Church there.' He pointed to a steeple that soared over the rooftops – hard to miss indeed.

'That will take you to Market Street.' With a curt nod, he and Stuart strode off, followed by porters carrying their collection of Indian artefacts and luggage.

My presence was beginning to attract attention of the unwanted sort. My street sense, far more acute than my woodcraft, alerted me to two men lounging against a stack of barrels who were eyeing my horse. I threw Little Turtle's cloth on Sasakwa's back and, mounting her quickly, spurred her on with a kick. She trotted smartly away, for once not disgracing her rider.

It took me some time to find the right house in Market Street as Davies had neglected to mention that it was one of the longest roads in town. I was almost screaming with impatience when I finally rode up to a neat double-fronted house with white curtains at the windows. I peeped in at the ground floor. It was theirs all right: Johnny's drawing things were scattered over the table and one of his jackets hung on the back of the chair. Windows were open on the upper floors so I hoped that meant someone was in.

I looked down at myself: I was filthy and dressed like an Indian – feathers, beads, bow and arrow. Laughing for the first time in weeks, I lifted the knocker.

A maid opened the door – and shut it again smartly.

I wrapped the knocker again loudly. 'No! You can't do that! It's me – it's Cat!' I thumped my fists on the door, ready to weep at this final barrier. 'Let me in!'

I could hear feet running down the stairs. The door flew open and Pedro stood in the entrance, Lizzie behind him. They both stared at me in astonishment for a fraction of a second before she shrieked and Pedro yelled:

'Cat!'

Grinning now, I asked meekly, gesturing to Sasakwa and myself, 'Weren't you expecting us?'

'What? How?' spluttered Pedro. Abandoning his questions, he hugged me close.

Lizzie sank on a bench. Watching over Pedro's shoulder, I suddenly realized she was about twice her normal girth.

'Lizzie, are you all right?' I asked anxiously, cursing myself for having sprung my arrival on her so thoughtlessly. I pushed Pedro gently away and knelt at her feet.

'Yes, I am – we are.' She patted her stomach. 'It's just . . . just a shock. We thought you might be dead and . . . and that's been hard enough to bear, but now –'

'Now you have to bear the fact that I've turned up to scandalize your neighbours?'

She pulled me to her and kissed my cheek. 'Don't be such a silly goose. I'm delighted you did. They have nothing sensible to talk about most of the time.' With a tearful smile crinkling her eyes, she put her forehead against mine and just held me there. Then she gave a sniff. 'But I forget myself – you must be exhausted. Pedro, can you call Greerson to see to the pony?'

'I must see to her first myself,' I said, remembering my promise to Tecumseh. Then it struck me. 'But Pedro, if you're here, does that mean Frank and Syd are too? Where are they? How did you get off the *Courageous*?' I burst out.

There were so many things I wanted to know.

Pedro had finally gathered his scattered wits. 'Yes, we're all here. They've gone with Johnny to the City Tavern – there's an assembly this evening.'

'What! They're out at a party!' A little part – all right, a big part – of me complained that this didn't seem very fitting when they should be agonizing about my fate.

Pedro smiled, guessing my thoughts. 'They've gone to appeal to the city fathers to aid them in the search for you. All of Philadelphia will be there tonight. Mr Dixon arrived yesterday from London with funds for an expedition to find you and they've –'

'Mr Dixon is here!'

'Yes, of course,' said Lizzie, stroking my arm as if she didn't want to let me go. 'My parents sent him to assist Frank as soon as they received word of what had happened to you. Frank sailed from Kingston to meet up with him; he arrived with Syd and Pedro only last week. We've been in uproar ever since.'

'Yes,' continued Pedro, 'we've been fitting out a

ship to return to Fort Frederica but were sadly short of money until Mr Dixon arrived –'

I had heard enough.

'Come on, Pedro, we're going.'

I mounted Sasakwa and held out a hand to him. Pedro and Lizzie exchanged confused glances.

'Going where?' he asked. 'You've only just arrived!'

'To save Frank from Dixon. Where else? Lizzie, put the water on for a hot bath, will you? We'll be back soon. And whatever you do, do not let your cousin anywhere near you while we're gone.'

Carried along by the firmness of my purpose, Pedro jumped up behind me.

'I suppose there's method to your madness, Cat?'

'Absolutely.'

He steered me southwards. 'And are you going to tell me what this is all about?'

'Of course. But first we've got to catch ourselves a rat.'

Lizzie had not exaggerated when she said all

Philadelphia was at the City Tavern that night. A line of coaches stretched the length of two blocks and the door was crowded with finely dressed ladies and gentlemen. Two flambeaux lit the entrance, fire leaping into the sky as the high society tribe met for their ceremonial dance.

'Look, Cat,' reasoned Pedro as I pulled Sasakwa to a halt opposite the entrance. 'The footmen won't let us in – not a black boy and . . . well, you look most peculiar.'

My rage against Dixon hummed in my ears; he was in there, only feet away from us. This couldn't wait.

'Where's the assembly room?' I asked.

'Straight ahead.' He pointed through the doors. We could hear the music from here, a full orchestra playing a country dance.

'Well, as we don't have an invitation, we'll just have to improvise.'

I spurred Sasakwa on. Game for anything that involved mischief, the horse leapt forward and trotted determinedly towards the shallow flight of steps at the entrance.

'You're not . . .?' groaned Pedro.

'I am,' I replied tight-lipped. I could see nothing for it but to force entry.

The flower of Philadelphian society screamed and jumped out of our way as we clattered through the door.

'Duck!' I ordered Pedro as we passed under the lintel.

Sasakwa's hooves echoed in the passageway, but she had spotted a banquet laid out directly in front of us and followed her nose. Footmen tried to step in our way and grab the bridle but she had had months of avoiding capture so knew how to handle them. One ended up in a potted plant, the other stretched on his stomach. I couldn't believe I was doing this: charging my way into a Society gathering on horseback! But I was committed now to my desperate resolution to get Dixon away from Frank. Bursting into the ballroom, Sasakwa scattered the dancers like ninepins and came to a halt at a tower of exotic fruits. I pulled her round; there was plenty of time for her to graze once I'd found Dixon.

The ladies had scurried to the side, fearing for their finery – and possibly afraid of me. I suppose I did look rather warlike in my outfit. The gentlemen had regrouped after the initial shock of my entry and were closing in. I didn't have long.

'Dixon!' I yelled my challenge as the orchestra ground to a ragged halt. 'Where are you?'

'Cat! My God, it *is* you!' I heard Frank's familiar voice to my left. I spun round. He was standing with a group of older gentlemen, Johnny and Syd at his shoulder, Dixon a few paces off. 'Where've you been?'

'Excuse me!' I pushed through the crowd and reined Sasakwa to a stop in front of my quarry.

'Cat, what on earth are you doing?' Johnny rushed forward and caught the horse's bridle.

'Rat-catching, Johnny, like a good cat should.' My tone was tight with fury. Johnny gave me a keen look; he was already working it out for himself.

Stepping towards me, Dixon's face was white but he managed to keep his voice steady. 'My dear girl, we are pleased and, may I say, relieved to see you, but have you lost your senses coming in here like this?' He gave the city fathers an apologetic look. 'This is the young woman we were speaking of; we can call the search off.' He gave a false laugh which no one joined.

A footman had now reached me and I felt a firm hand grasp my leg. I was about to be removed from Sasakwa's back, losing my chance to denounce Dixon publicly. Seeing this, Syd pushed his way through the crowd and pulled the servant off. I put my hand on his shoulder in thanks and turned to address Frank.

'Frank, it was your cousin all along. He faked the attack. He only pretended to be injured. Maclean told me all about it.'

My friend gave Dixon an anguished glance; his cousin shook his head slightly, rolling his eyes in my direction.

'It's true; I swear it!'

'She's obviously unhinged by her ordeal, Frank,' said Dixon, putting an arm around him. 'Let's take her home before she causes any more scandal. Our family has suffered enough.'

'Ask him to show you his scar,' I continued

loudly. 'A bad cut to the belly should leave some mark.'

Dixon let go of Frank and rounded on me. 'Don't be preposterous!'

Johnny caught on quickly. 'What have you to hide, sir?' he asked.

'Display a scar in front of this company!' Dixon protested. 'You may have lost all sense of decency, Fitzroy, but I have not.'

His indignation was almost convincing. Frank met my eyes, then turned to his cousin, pushing his arm away as Dixon attempted to steer him from the room.

'Show me your scar, Will,' he said quietly.

The room fell ominously silent.

Dixon flushed with anger, but he was also afraid. He pointed at me, his finger shaking. 'You can't listen to the wild accusations of this . . . this base-born female!'

Frank's face hardened. He knew.

'So Cat's right: it *was* you. How . . . how could you, Will?'

Dixon squared his shoulders, realizing the

game was up. 'I don't have to answer to you for my actions! What do you know of struggling to survive? You with the privileges of rank and riches dropping into your lap, unearned, unappreciated!'

Frank frowned and drew himself up to his full height; he now had an inch on his cousin and a lot more hard-earned muscle. 'I know all about survival, thanks to the education you saw fit to give me in His Majesty's Navy. Did you not know that if you had asked, I would have done everything in my power to help you?'

'Charity?' spat Dixon. 'I didn't want to live in debt to you.'

'So instead you stooped to *this*?' Frank looked at his cousin in disgust. 'For what you did to me, I pardon you; but what you did to my friends, to Cat especially, that I'll never forgive.' He was white with fury. 'You forced a girl to taste hell to further your own interests. You are despicable!'

Dixon gave me a contemptuous glare. 'You take offence for her? A girl you picked off the streets, a nobody?'

Frank threw a punch that hit Dixon squarely on the jaw. He crumpled to the floor.

'Never come near me again,' Frank said, standing over his cousin, his knuckles reddened by the blow. 'If you dare show your face, you'll regret it. Now go!'

Dixon picked himself up shakily. He tried to brush himself down and regain a little dignity.

'You have no respect for the honour of our family,' Dixon said in a shrill voice. 'You will pull us all down into the dirt with the gutter creatures you prefer. Someone had to try and stop you but I regret you have not learned your lesson. You will live to rue the day that you took up with these people, cousin.'

'At least I'll live,' Frank snarled. 'And don't try and pretend you did this for the good of the family; you did it for yourself. If you'd had your way, I'd be dead, so I suggest you beat a hasty retreat before I change my mind and have you arrested.'

Wiping blood from his chin, Dixon pushed through the crowd and disappeared into the night.

There was a profound, embarrassed silence.

The city elders knew not how to restore the assembly now it had been so rudely gatecrashed. Johnny was struggling to find some placatory words but for once they would not come. But Frank was at no such loss. He held out his hand to help me dismount. Sasakwa wandered off to the buffet table, treading on several costly gowns in the process, and was soon happily investigating the hot-house flowers. Frank said nothing but gathered me into his arms and hugged me; then Syd made a third to our little huddle, so that Frank and I were lifted off our feet. We parted red-faced and rumpled. Johnny stepped forward and ruffled my hair, coming away with a turkey feather that he stuck behind his ear with a wink.

Frank took a look around our crowd of well-dressed spectators and gave me a roguish grin. He bowed.

'Things appear to be at something of a stand. Miss Royal, would you do me the honour of the next dance?'

'You're joking?' I took a step back. 'What – dressed like this?' I gestured to my rows of beads and belted green shirt with silver coins.

'Yes, dressed like that, but perhaps without the bow and arrows.' He removed my weapons and handed them to Syd. 'Music, please.' He waved to the conductor but the man was still frozen with shock.

Pedro elbowed his way over to the orchestra and commandeered a violin off the nearest musician. With a smile at us, he struck up a minuet.

Frank saw my hesitation. 'Do you care to join me or do Indian maids not know how to dance?'

'Of course we do.' I curtseyed, hand curved elegantly to my breast. 'Every savage can dance.'

Syd gave a guffaw of laughter and slapped me on the back. 'Go on, Kitten, show these Yankees 'ow to do it then,' he said, beaming. 'As long as you let me 'ave the next dance.'

Frank took my fingers lightly in his and we began to walk through the steps of the minuet. Strangely, no one else saw fit to join this set but stood aloof. Frank's eyes sparkled as he took in my attire.

'I can see that you have an interesting tale to

tell,' he murmured. 'I can't wait to hear it.'

'On the condition you let me get my version in first, before you get a garbled one from Mr Davies, our intrepid explorer.'

Frank squeezed my hand. 'I can't tell you how relieved I am to find you still in the land of the living, Cat.'

'I'm rather glad myself.'

Smiling at the scandalized faces surrounding us, Frank dipped with polish ease as I stepped lightly round him, our hands still clasped.

'I always said you would make a fine dancer, in silk or buckskin,' Frank murmured in my ear as we progressed up the hall once more. 'We may have had to travel to the New World to do it, but I am proud to be dancing with you at last, Miss Royal.'

EPILOGUE

GOD-DAUGHTER

Two weeks later, I stood in the sunshine in an upper room of Johnny and Lizzie's house, holding a mewling bundle in my arms. Lizzie was collapsed on to the pillow, snuggled up in fresh sheets and clean nightgown, taking a well-earned rest. I hadn't realized having a baby was so hard.

'Lovely, isn't she?' Lizzie murmured.

'Perfect,' I agreed. 'Shall I tell the proud father that he can come up?'

She nodded and gave me a tired smile. 'I hope he's all right.'

'You are worrying about *him*!' I marvelled, shifting the baby into a comfortable crook in my arm. 'If I know Frank, Pedro and Syd, they will have plied him with brandy for the past twelve hours. I doubt he will be still standing.'

The men summoned, far more sober than I expected, I moved to join Syd and Pedro in the doorway as Johnny and Frank gathered around Lizzie's bed. Johnny's face was a picture – a mixture of joy and terror as he held his tiny daughter and touched her exquisite feet.

'Is Lady Elizabeth well?' Syd asked delicately, putting an arm around my shoulders.

'Yes, she's fine now, though it was worse than a storm at sea giving life to that armful of trouble.'

Syd and Pedro looked at Lizzie in awe.

'Put me off having children, I can tell you,' I added.

The baby squawked and batted Johnny on the nose, flailing out for the breast.

'Do you know what? She reminds me of someone,' Johnny said. 'Boisterous, demanding, making a noisy entrance into the world.'

'Indeed,' said Lizzie, with a tired smile. 'Takes after her godmother. Perhaps we should name her after her too?'

'Just what I was thinking, my love,' agreed Johnny. 'So, what do you say, Cat?'

'What?' I took a step back into Syd in surprise.

'Catherine Elizabeth Fitzroy: not a bad name with which to start life. That's if her godmother will let us borrow it.' Johnny felt for his wife's hand and pressed it to his lips.

My heart filled with pride as I realized they were talking about me. I took the wooden carving of the fish from around my neck and moved to hang it on the baby's swinging crib so she would see it whenever she was awake. 'I, Cat Royal of Drury Lane, and of the Wind Clan, would be delighted to sponsor her.' I said the words solemnly, meaning every syllable. I then turned back to my friends with a grin. 'After all, with two such perfect parents, someone's got to set an example to her of how not to behave.'

Curtain falls

CAT'S GLOSSARY

BELAY – disregard, stop or make fast

BELAYING PIN – wooden bar on ship's rail to which ropes can be fastened

BICORNE – two-cornered hat

BOSUN – also boatswain, officer responsible for sails, rigging and tackle

BOSUN'S MATE – seaman who helps the bosun execute orders, often with the aid of a rope on your back

BOW – foremost part of the ship's hull

BOW STREET RUNNERS – London law enforcers

BULKHEAD – upright partition in a ship

CANTING CREW – thieves bound together by their own language

CITY TAVERN – social hub of Philadelphia

COTILLION – lively French dance, requiring all eight dancers to take part at same time, leaving much room for mistakes

CROSS-TREES – junction of mast with yardarm, lookout point

DOXY, DOXIES (pl.) – unflattering description of a woman

FLAMBEAU – a flaming torch

FLASH MORT – rich, showy girl

FLIES – highest point above stage where scenery can be suspended

FLING ONE'S HAT AFTER SOMEONE – make a futile pursuit

FORT FREDERICA – abandoned fort on St Simon's Island, Georgia

GROG – watered-down spirits (or spirited-up water, depending on your point of view)

GUNNER – officer responsible for ship's heavy guns

HALYARD – rope used to hoist a sail

HEADS – very unprivate privy on board ship below figurehead

HOLD – lowest space in a ship, below all decks

HOLYSTONE – sandstone used to scour deck

LARBOARD – left-hand side if you are facing the bow

LINK BOYS – boys and men who are hired to light your way to and from evening entertainments

MASTER – on a ship, the officer responsible for navigation and piloting

MASTHEAD – lookout point on top of mast

MESS – the group of people you eat with on board

MESS KID – rope-handled bowl used to distribute food

MINUET – slow, very elegant dance with little steps

MIZZEN – mast at back of ship

MUDLARKING – scavenging on the banks of the Thames, a smelly but occasionally rewarding business

PHILADELPHIA – a major city port in America

PRESS GANG – enforced recruiting agency for the navy not known for their subtlety

PUMP ROOM – place in Bath for taking the waters and showing your finery

PURSER – officer responsible for victuals

QUARTERDECK – deck above main deck at back of boat (are you following this?)

REEF – a tuck in a sail or (more ominously) rocks below water

SAVANNAH – open plains

SHROUDS – ropes supporting the mast from the side, rope ladders

SKILLYGALEE – oatmeal gruel cooked in fatty water

(is your mouth watering? I thought not)

SKYLARKING – playing in the rigging (you have to be mad to like it)

SLOOP – cutter-rigged (one-mast) coasting vessel (don't worry about it – it's a kind of boat, that's all you really need to know)

STARBOARD – right-hand side if you are facing the bow

STERN – back end of the boat

STEVEDORE – man who loads and unloads ships

SWABBING – more or less the same as the landlubber's scrubbing

TOP GALLANTS – a square sail set above the topsail, the highest one of all (and not a bunch of swell gents as you might think)

TOP MEN – elite crew who rig the highest sails

UPPER ROOMS – new Assembly Rooms in Bath, place to see and be seen

WEEVILS – small beetles that infest food

YARDARM – horizontal spar (or pole to you and me) holding sails

YOUNG BLOOD – rich young gentleman, sporting type

KANAWHA'S GLOSSARY

CHICKAMAUGA – dwelling place of the chief

ENHESSE – friend

ENKA – all right, yes

ESTONKO – hello, how are you?

FO – Bee

HELES-HAYV – medicine maker

HERES CE – hello

PUSE – grandmother

SASAKWA – goose

VHOYVKETS – let's go

WELEETKA – running water

YOPO – nose

THE NEXT CAT ROYAL
ADVENTURE

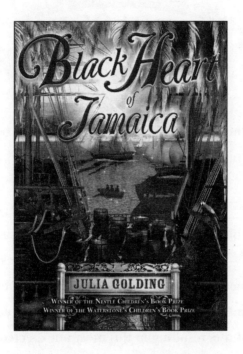

Black Heart of Jamaica . . . In which Cat turns pirate,
undertakes a Caribbean Cruise and gets mixed up in
a slave revolt. Cat's most outrageous adventure yet!

PREPARE TO SWASH YOUR BUCKLE!

Philadelphia, United States of America,
June 1792 – Curtain rises.

PROLOGUE

AUDITIONS

This is the story of how I, Cat Royal, became a pirate.

Reader, before you throw up your hands in horror at this scandalous confession or call the constable, I rush to assure you that my piracy was entirely accidental. When my adventures in the Caribbean began, I had absolutely no intention of pursuing this path; unfortunately events conspired against me, resulting in this most unexpected twist of fate.

The beginnings of my West Indian tale were impeccably correct, which makes the descent into piracy even more surprising, not least to myself. It began with the search for employment. Having foiled a plot to do away with Lord Francis, the son of the

Duke of Avon, my friends and I had ended up in Philadelphia on the east coast of America.* It was now high time I decided what to do with my future. Should I head home to England with Lord Francis (that's Frank to you and me) and Syd, both of whom had their lives to resume after the unplanned adventure aboard His Majesty's ship *Courageous*? Or should I stay in America with Frank's sister, Lizzie, and her husband, Johnny? As the weeks passed, I realized that I had no desire to be at a loose end in their household. Quite understandably, they were absorbed in each other and their newborn and did not need me underfoot. But neither was I ready yet to return home to England. I felt as if my true life waited but I was not sure where.

'Cat, if you're determined to work,' declared Frank as we sat in the parlour of his sister's snug little house on Market Street one sunny afternoon, 'you'll need to decide on a career.'

He was a pretty sight, nursing his one-month-old niece on his shoulder as her tiny fists gripped a lock

* For full details of that fiendish plot, see my fourth adventure, *Cat O'Nine Tails*.

of his curly dark hair. With his long limbs and twinkling blue eyes, I predicted that my noble friend would break many hearts on his return to England – particularly if they saw how good he was in the nursery. The Mamas would be moving heaven and earth to wed their daughters to one of England's most eligible young bachelors.

Yet while his future was certain – to be the fox to all the husband-hunting debutantes for the next few years – mine was far less settled.

'But what can I do?' I asked, throwing aside the newspaper. I'd been skimming it for news of the revolution in France.

'Well, let me think.' Frank gave me a smug smile as little Catherine drifted off to sleep under his soothing touch. 'You can pretend to be a boy convincingly, you dance well, sing passably, write amusingly; I've seen you climb the rigging like a seasoned salt, and ride bareback like a native – Cat, there really is no end to your talents. And you also speak at least two foreign languages.'

Entering from the kitchen, Lizzie kissed her brother on the top of the head; Johnny followed carrying the tea tray.

'You've a masterful touch with babies, Frank,' she commended her brother. 'What I shame I can't hire you as a nursemaid.'

Lizzie looked very pretty with her long chestnut locks caught up in a practical chignon and a white apron protecting her light blue day dress. Her new role as American wife and mother was quite a climb down from her days as a British duke's daughter with hundreds of servants at her beck and call, but the change seemed to suit her. She'd never been one to stand on ceremony; after all, she had befriended me.

'Sorry, Lizzie, but as much as such skills are worthy of a duke-in-training, I feel a perverse desire to take up my place at Cambridge instead.' Frank rubbed his cheek against the soft hair of the baby. 'Tempting though the offer is.'

'And Father wants you to assume your proper title now you're at an age to go out into society,' Lizzie reminded him.

Frank groaned.

'The Earl of Arden?' I prompted, remembering his title from our time in Bath.

'I much prefer "Frank" but it won't do back home.' Frank sighed at the thought. 'Mama delayed the day as long as possible for me but now I'll have to resign myself to answering to a name that sounds like a coaching inn.'

'A very superior coaching inn,' I consoled him. 'Do you want me to call you Arden, or would you prefer Lord Dog and Duck, or perhaps Lord Jolly Boatman?'

He chuckled. 'None of the above, thank you, Cat. And the day you refer to me as Arden is the day I start calling you Miss Royal. I insist that you at least stick with Frank.'

The matter of titles settled to our mutual satisfaction, Johnny returned to the conversation that had been interrupted by the entry of the tea service.

'So what were you saying to Cat about talents?' he asked as I cleared a space for the tray among the litter of his drawing things.

I rolled my eyes. 'Frank seeks to persuade me that I am eminently employable.'

To my surprise, Lizzie nodded her agreement. 'Quite right too. You have many skills; you just need to find a suitable situation.'

'Not that you have to work,' Frank chipped in. 'You know my parents will look after you.'

My pride bristled at the suggestion. 'I don't need looking after – well, not much,' I added, remembering how the Avons had taken me in after Drury Lane had been demolished.

Johnny chuckled. 'I'm sure you don't, Catkin. You are a very capable young lady – you've proved that on the high seas and in the wilds of America. But you should also know that you are welcome to stay here as long as you have need.'

'And don't forget that Syd wants you to go home with him,' Frank said quietly for my ears only as Lizzie rattled the tea cups.

I knew full well what he meant. Syd, my oldest friend from Covent Garden, was determined not to let me out of his sight again, not since I had jumped ship from under his nose and given him months of heartache when he believed me lost for good. But his plans for me led to a future marriage and life as a butcher's wife, something I was not remotely ready to consider – not yet anyway.

'I'm sorry, but I don't want to be wrapped in cotton wool and that's exactly what Syd will do to me; I want to stand on my own two feet – prove to myself that I can make my own way.'

Lizzie poured the tea with efficient grace. 'Speaking of which, where are Syd and Pedro?'

'At the docks,' said Frank, helping himself to a biscuit that he somehow managed to eat without getting crumbs on Catherine. 'I asked them to find out which ships are in harbour. If I'm to go up in Michaelmas term, I have to leave as soon as possible.'

'And what about Pedro? Has he decided to go too?' Johnny asked, toying with his pen. His long fingers never bearing to be idle for long, he picked up a piece of paper and began to sketch his brother-in-law with his baby daughter.

'He's waiting for Cat's decision,' Frank replied. 'Make sure you catch my best side, Johnny.'

'You don't have one, Lord Dog and Duck,' Johnny replied with a wink at me. He was taking his role of teasing older brother-in-law to heart. 'So, Catkin, what's it to be?'

I spread my hands empty in front of me. 'Any

suggestions?'

'You're far too young for a governess,' mused Lizzie as she stirred cream into her tea.

'And the strain of behaving would probably kill you,' muttered Frank. Lizzie swatted his leg, but from her smile I could tell she agreed. For that matter, so did I.

'I would've thought the answer was fairly obvious,' said Johnny, scrutinizing his quick drawing.

What could he mean? There were few professions open to women: teacher, maid . . .

'Surely not a seamstress!' I gasped.

'No!' my three friends said in unison. Then we all laughed. My sewing skills were infamous.

Johnny laid aside his portrait and flipped the newspaper over to the classified advertisements. He pointed to an announcement with the end of his pen. 'Take a look at that. You have years of experience at Drury Lane, Cat. A theatrical company here would welcome you with open arms.'

I studied the page. Philadelphia had a lively social scene with a number of companies providing drama and musical entertainments. Indeed, only last week I had been to a passable production of Dryden's *All for Love*. Now it seemed that one of those companies was taking on new members:

The Peabody Theatrical
Ensemble

Is proud to

Announce its Summer Tour

Engagements already secured in the West Indies.
Ladies and Gentlemen of outstanding
abilities sought.
Recruiting now.

It sounded very grand, but I had my suspicions. Even the top theatres of the world like Drury Lane and Covent Garden were somewhat – all right, *very* – moth-eaten when examined in the light of day. This ensemble was likely to be three stage-struck fools and a cart of props. I read the advertisement again with greater care. Or perhaps not. If they already had engagements organized abroad, that suggested proper management: the Peabody Ensemble might be worth a closer look.

'You think they'll take me on?' I asked dubiously.

'I'm sure you stand an excellent chance,' Johnny confirmed. 'You have experience both on and off stage; you're just what a small company like that needs for a tour, able to turn your hand to anything. And it's not forever. It'll give you a taste of the life and you can make a final decision as to whether it's the career for you when you return here in the autumn.'

He was right. It was the perfect opportunity for me to test the waters. I had always seen my future as being bound up with the theatre, but the closure of Drury Lane had prematurely cut off those hopes. Now I had a chance to get back into that life.

My face must have betrayed my excitement for my friends exchanged pleased looks.

'Well, that's settled then,' said Frank, stroking the baby's back. Catherine gave a most unladylike burp. 'I imagine it will suit you down to the ground, but I hope you don't decide to stay away from England forever, Cat.'

'Just for a few months,' I reiterated hesitantly.

'Yes, that's right,' said Johnny, returning to his

sketch.

'A chance to find out if my talents really do lie on stage?'

'Absolutely,' nodded Frank. 'But I for one have no doubts on that score.'

'All you need to do now is persuade them to take you on,' concluded Lizzie.

Easier said than done.

'That won't be difficult.' Pedro had returned unnoticed and must have been listening from the doorway. He leaned against the jamb, his arms crossed, fingers tapping restlessly as if itching to return to his instrument.

'I'm pleased you have so much faith in me,' I smiled.

'That wasn't what I meant.' Pedro took a step towards the sofa and leant across Frank to steal a biscuit. He waved it in the air like a baton. 'Not that I don't have faith in you, of course.'

'Thanks.'

'But if we offer ourselves as a duet – you with your talents and me with mine – then I doubt they'll be able to resist.'

I jumped up and hugged him, making him drop his biscuit. 'You'll come with me?'

He hugged me back. 'Of course. You're not getting rid of me so easily, Cat Royal. Not this time.'

My grin must have stretched from ear to ear. The future seemed far less daunting when not faced alone.

'If they turn down the best violinist in the world, and the star of the Paris Opera,' I performed a perfect pirouette, dipping into a curtsey, 'then they are not worthy of us.'

'That's the spirit,' agreed Pedro, rubbing his hands together. 'So when do we start?'

The auditions took place in the Man Full of Trouble Tavern on Little Dock Creek, a humble inn that offered not much more than warm beer and warm beds to sailors passing through port. The Peabody Ensemble had to cut their cloth to suit their purse and I took this as due warning that this was going to be no luxury theatrical cruise of the West Indies. Yet the modesty of the surroundings did not deter those dreaming of stardom. As we approached we found that a line of hopefuls already stretched around the block. Though I had never joined one before, I'd seen such queues in Drury Lane – gatherings of the talentless multitude and the talented few, all desperate for their moment centre stage. My confidence took a little dent: with so many trying for a place, would we really be so irresistible? Shoulders back, head up, I steeled myself for the ordeal. We would never find out unless we tried.

Pedro and I attached ourselves to the end of the queue, resigned to a long wait. Syd stood with us, frowning at an inept juggler practising a few places in front. My boxing friend attracted admiring glances from the girls thanks to his muscular frame and handsome – if a little battered – face, but today he was oblivious to them.

'Are you sure about this, Cat?' he grumbled, rubbing his chin. He hated the idea that I intended to stay in the Americas without him. I knew that, if he hadn't had a swindling boxing manager to pursue, he would have abandoned his plans to go home.

'I'm sure, Syd.'

'And you'll come 'ome when you've done this tour?' The anxious note in his voice made my heart ache for him. He was so desperate not to lose me forever, but what could I say when I didn't know what was going to happen?

'I make no promises, Syd. There's nothing for me in London now Drury Lane is closed.'

'Nothink, Cat? There's me – and the lads.'

I squeezed his hand. I could at least provide him with some comfort.

'Syd, I can't imagine living the rest of my life away from London. No doubt I'll be drawn back one day. It's my home after all.'

He nodded.

I tugged on his waistcoat to get his full attention. 'But you promise not to wait for me? It might be years before I return.'

He refused to meet my eyes, instead gazing fixedly at an advert for McLackland's toothpowder. 'What I decide to do is my own business,' he said stiffly – meaning he fully intended to wait.

'Next!' bellowed a man taking names at the door. Pedro and I shuffled forward a pace. I glanced back but Syd had disappeared into the crowd.

'Pedro Amakye, violinist and dancer, and

Catherine Royal, actress, singer and dancer,' Pedro informed him.

The man raised an eyebrow at us both, hearing the unusual accents.

'Both from Drury Lane, London,' Pedro finished.

The man's eyes lit up. 'Well now, ain't that just fine and dandy. I was thinking you'd say you were from Africa.' He eyed Pedro speculatively, taking in the contrary signals of his dark skin coupled with fine clothes. 'My, my, Drury Lane. Mrs Peabody sure will be pleased to meet you two. Go on in, boy.'

Mrs Peabody – now that was a surprise. A woman running a theatre company? She had my immediate respect.

We stepped into the audition room. The juggler had just been summarily dismissed and a pale-faced girl had taken his place.

'Name?' barked a woman seated by the pianoforte.

'Charlotte Potter, Mrs Peabody,' the girl whispered, intimidated by the grim-faced lady of indeterminate years who was glaring at her. Dressed in black, the company manager looked rather like a bald eagle poised to swoop on any theatrical failing, ready to rip reputations to shreds.

'Go on then, Miss Potter, do your worst.' Mrs Peabody nodded to the accompanist. The pianoforte began to tinkle. The girl opened her mouth to sing a ballad in a quavering voice.

The response was ruthless.

'Next!' bellowed Mrs Peabody. 'I suggest you try another profession, Miss Potter, one that doesn't involve singing, and stop wasting my time.'

The poor girl was led away in tears. Mrs Peabody might be worthy of respect but she also inspired in me a creeping case of stage fright. I glanced nervously at Pedro, but he seemed unruffled by the humiliations inflicted on others – so secure was he in his own talent.

'Who are you?' Mrs Peabody enquired with an exasperated sigh as Pedro and I made our way forward. She was evidently tired of the whole business after a morning of disappointment. I was tempted to slip away without trying her patience further.

Before we could introduce ourselves, the man who had greeted us at the door called out:

'Thought you'd like to know, ma'am, they're from Drury Lane.'

Mrs Peabody's face relaxed into an unexpectedly fond smile. 'Ah, Drury Lane!' She waved her notes languidly in front of her face as if the memory had summoned up a warm flush. 'My, my. I was once Mr Garrick's favourite, did you know? Miss Dorothea Featherstone, famed for my Desdemona and Cleopatra.'

Strange, I'd never heard of a Miss Featherstone and I thought I knew all the names of the great actresses of the past.

'He said no one could match my deportment and diction. My success was certain. That was before I married the late Mr Peabody, of course.' Her mouth wrinkled into a bitter line.

Pedro and I exchanged looks.

Mrs Peabody flapped the memories away. 'Well, well, let's see what you can do then,' and she sat back to judge our pieces.

Pedro went first. To begin with those waiting in the queue did not give a black boy the courtesy of silence, chatting and laughing loudly at the side of the audition room. That was until he completed his first musical phrase. I was delighted to note the open mouths and pleasantly shocked expressions as the lively piece by Bach wove its spell. Pedro finished to an awed hush, then enthusiastic applause.

'I think he's hired,' muttered the rejected juggler in my ear, not sounding the least bit jealous. 'She'd be a fool not to snap him up – and Mrs Peabody is no one's fool.'

I nodded politely but could not answer as nerves had set in: my turn. I couldn't let Pedro down.

My friend gave me a grin, summoning me forward.

Imagine you're back on the *Courageous*, I told myself. They're just shipmates wanting to be entertained.

So why did I feel more like a Christian about to be thrown to the lions?

Pedro ran through the introduction to *Blow the Man Down*. It was now or never. Taking a breath, I began to sing the sea shanty.

I cannot claim the instant success that followed Pedro's performance, but I sang my heart out. The superior quality of Pedro's playing always brought out the best in me. I slipped back into the familiar place with him – the easy partnership of music. As I made eye contact with my audience, I felt opinion shift in my favour. Many smiled, some tapped their toes, others gave me encouraging nods. When I finished I closed my eyes for a second, then turned to face my judge.

'Well, Miss Royal, I congratulate you: that was very sweetly done.'

My relief at her praise was greater than my pleasure.

Mrs Peabody's stern face cracked into a smile. 'Thank the Lord I haven't completely wasted my morning on nobodies without an ounce of talent!' 'At least there are two young people in Philadelphia with skills worthy of the Peabody Theatrical Ensemble. Report to Penn's Landing on Monday. We're sailing on the *Running Sally*. My stage manager will give you a list of what is required and settle your wages. I'm delighted you have joined us.' She waved us aside; and with a hunch of her shoulders, her bird-of-prey stance was back in place, ready for the next victim.